Maps for U.S. History
Map Resource Book

Artists: Pat St. Onge and Bill Beard
Editor: Mary Dieterich
Proofreader: April Albert

COPYRIGHT © 2016 Mark Twain Media, Inc.

ISBN 978-1-62223-592-6

Printing No. CD-404247

Mark Twain Media, Inc., Publishers
Distributed by Carson-Dellosa Publishing LLC

Visit us at www.carsondellosa.com

Table of Contents

Table of Contents (Cont.)

Introduction

    Maps for U.S. History provides teachers, parents, and students with a selection of high-quality maps for classroom and homeschool use. From the first exploration and settlement of the Americas to the post-Civil War years, these maps will complement your social studies curriculum as you study the history of the United States.

    These black and white maps are all reproducible for student use. They can also be made into transparencies or scanned into digital files for use with a classroom projection device. The ebook version includes some color maps, and the digital files are ready for printing or projection.

    This collection of maps provides handy resources for illustrating the geography of historical events, such as settlement, wars, trade, peace agreements, and territorial expansion. Students will be able to practice their geography skills by using the map keys to decipher symbols, discovering the landforms represented on the maps, and gauging distances using the map scales. Many of the maps are related, showing changes over time. Use the maps with your own curriculum in a variety of ways to reinforce the five themes of geography: location, place, region, movement, and human-environment interaction.

Name: _____

Date: _____

Land Bridge Theory

Legend:

Land bridge during the last ice age

Routes probably followed by the earliest Americans

SIBERIA

BERINGIA

Bering Strait

Bering Sea

NORTH AMERICA

Pacific Ocean

N E S W

Name: _____

Date: _____

Migration Patterns of Early Americans

Map #: 002

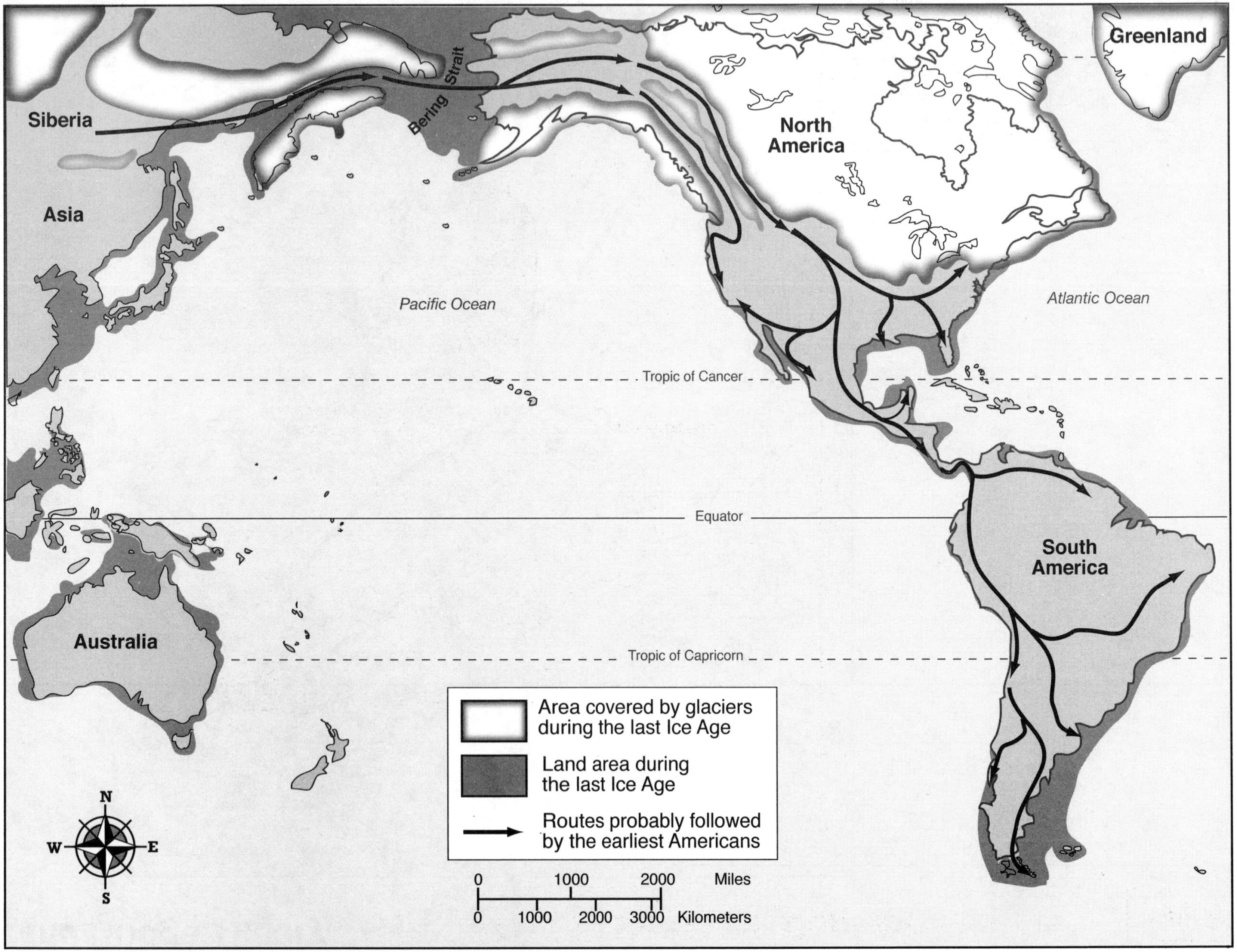

Greenland

North America

Atlantic Ocean

South America

Tropic of Cancer

Equator

Tropic of Capricorn

Pacific Ocean

Bering Strait

Siberia

Asia

Australia

Area covered by glaciers during the last Ice Age

Land area during the last Ice Age

Routes probably followed by the earliest Americans

Miles

Kilometers

0   1000   2000

0   1000   2000   3000

N   E   S   W

Name: _____

Date: _____

Map #: 003

The Mayas, Aztecs, and Incas Before European Contact

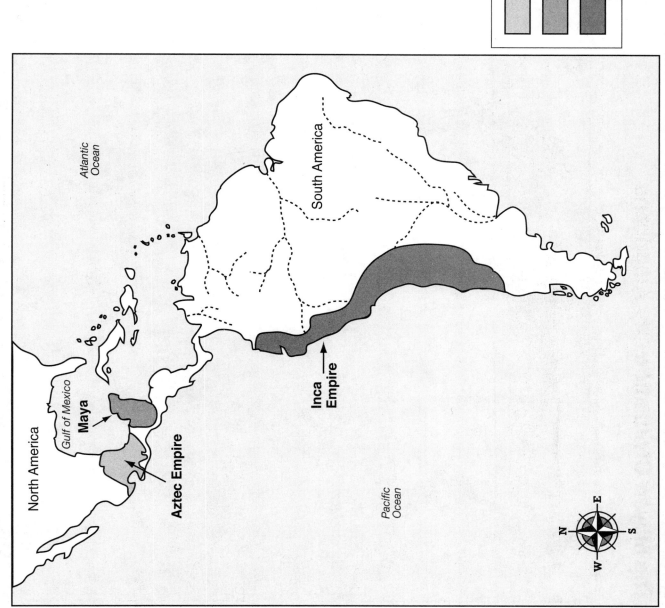

North America

Gulf of Mexico

Atlantic Ocean

Maya

Aztec Empire

South America

Inca Empire

Pacific Ocean

Aztec

Maya

Inca

N E S W

Name: ______________________ Date: ______________________

The Mayan Civilization

Map #: 004

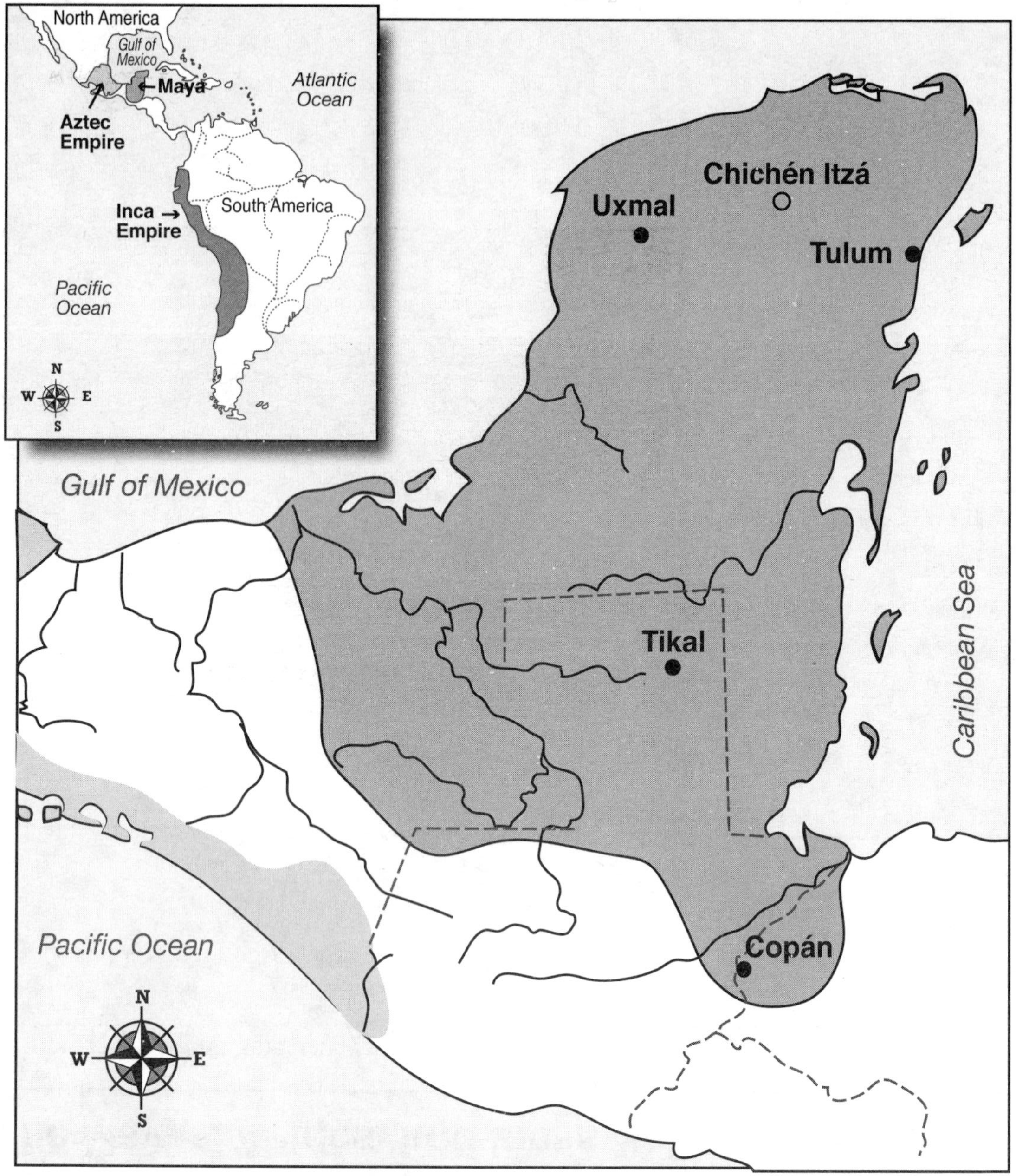
North America
Gulf of Mexico
Maya
Aztec Empire
Atlantic Ocean
Inca Empire
South America
Pacific Ocean
N
W
E
S
Gulf of Mexico
Uxmal
Chichén Itzá
Tulum
Tikal
Copán
Caribbean Sea
Pacific Ocean

Aztec
Maya
Inca
Territory Boundary
River

Name:

Date:

The Aztec Empire

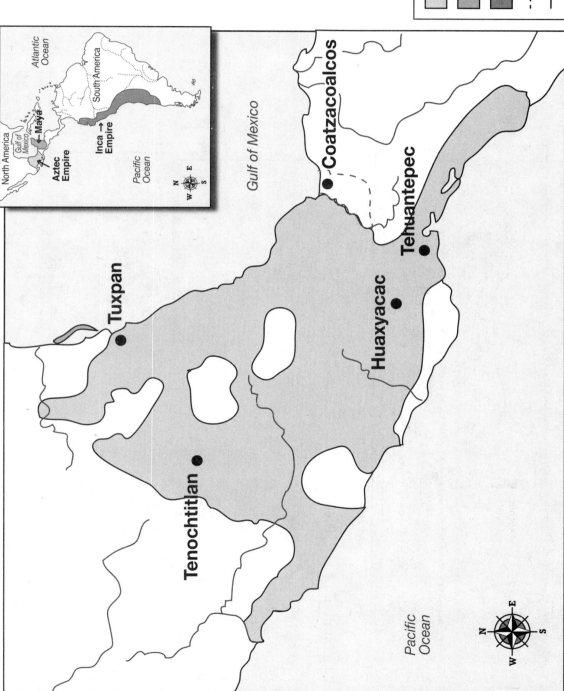

	Aztec
	Maya
	Inca
---	Territory Boundary
—	River

Name: _____

Date: _____

The Inca Empire

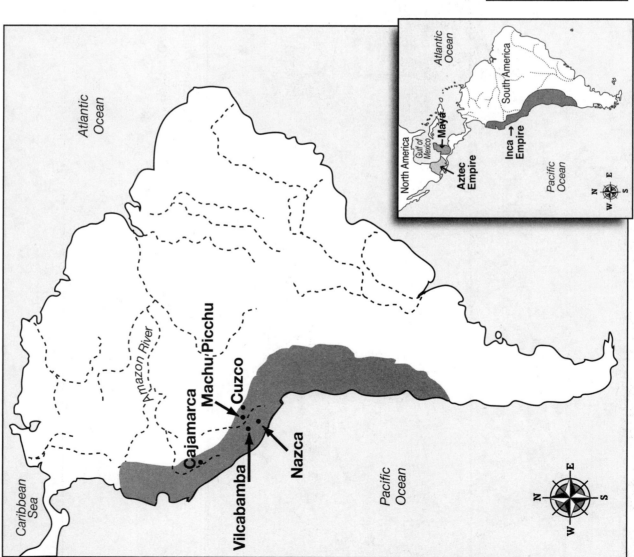

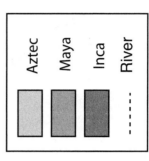

Name: _____

Date: _____

Ancient Cultures of the United States

Legend:
- Anasazi
- Hohokam
- Mound builders
- Area of most mounds

CANADA

Lake Superior
Lake Huron
Lake Michigan
Lake Erie
Lake Ontario

Atlantic Ocean

Etowah

Cahokia

Mesa Verde

Pueblo Bonita

Snaketown

Gulf of Mexico

MEXICO

Pacific Ocean

0   200   400 Miles
0   200   400   600 Kilometers

N E S W

Map #: 008

Name: _____

Date: _____

Native American Culture Groups With Tribe Names

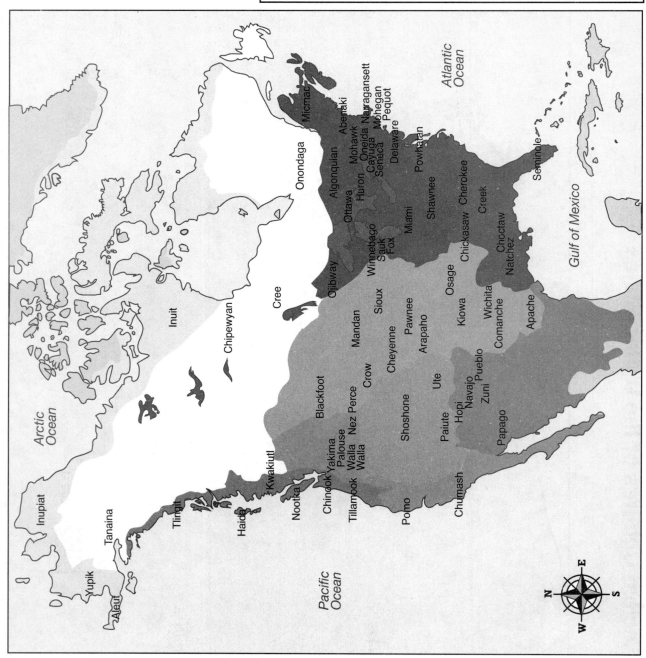

Culture Groups

- Arctic
- California
- Great Basin
- Northeast
- Northwest Coast
- Great Plains
- Plateau
- Southeast
- Southwest
- Subarctic

Name: _____

Date: _____

Voyages of Eric the Red and Leif Ericson

Map #: 009

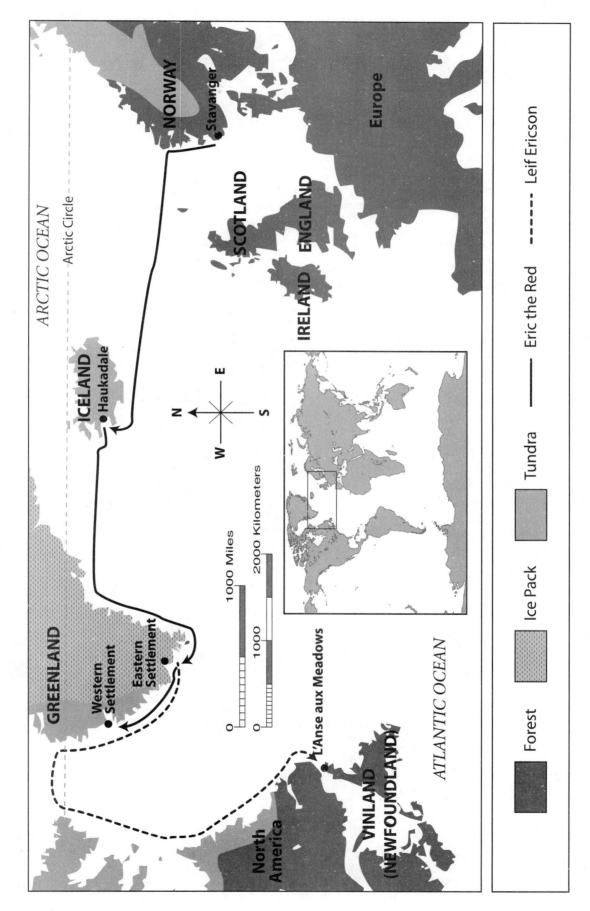

Name: _____ Date: _____

Trade Routes to Asia

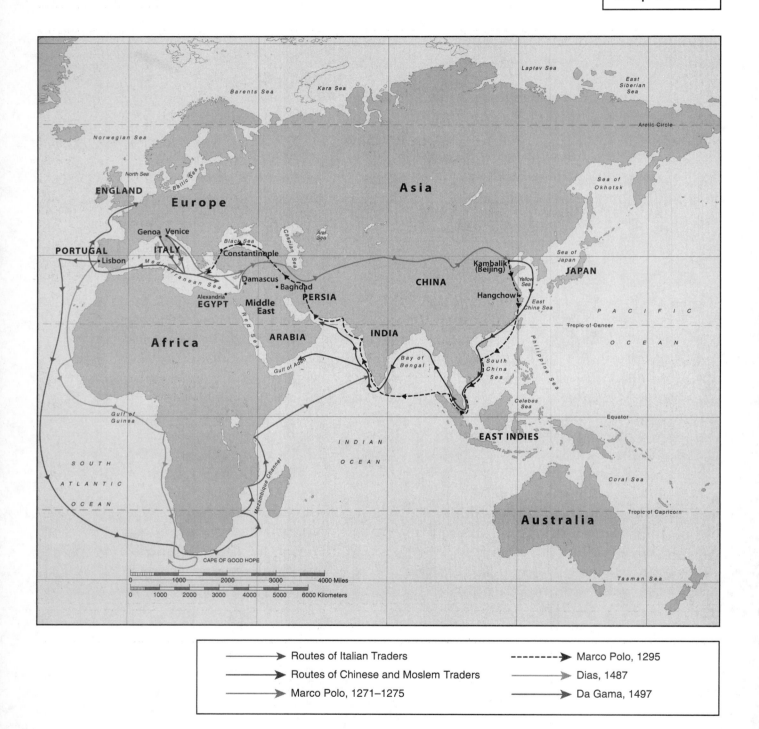

——→ Routes of Italian Traders	------→ Marco Polo, 1295
——→ Routes of Chinese and Moslem Traders	——→ Dias, 1487
——→ Marco Polo, 1271–1275	——→ Da Gama, 1497

Name: _____ Date: _____

The 1487 Voyage of Bartholomeu Dias

Map #: 011

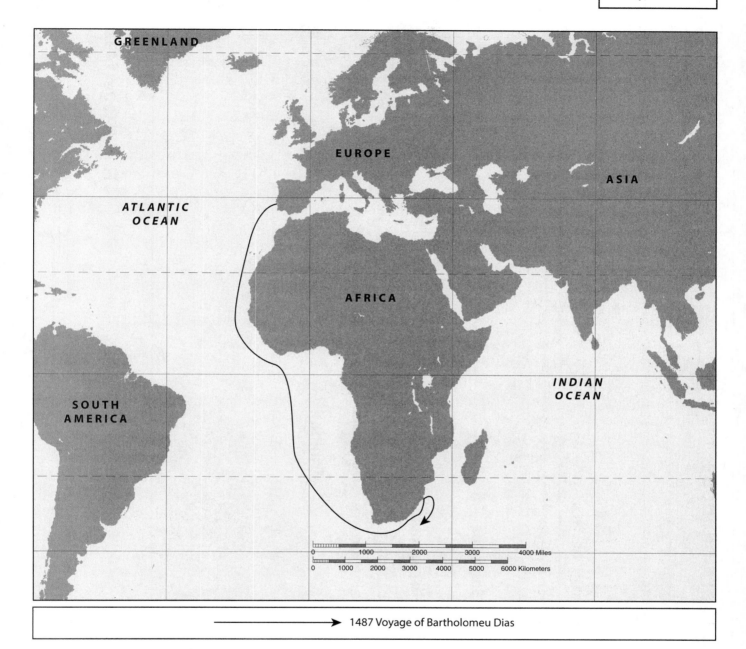

1487 Voyage of Bartholomeu Dias

Name: _____

Date: _____

The Four Voyages of Columbus

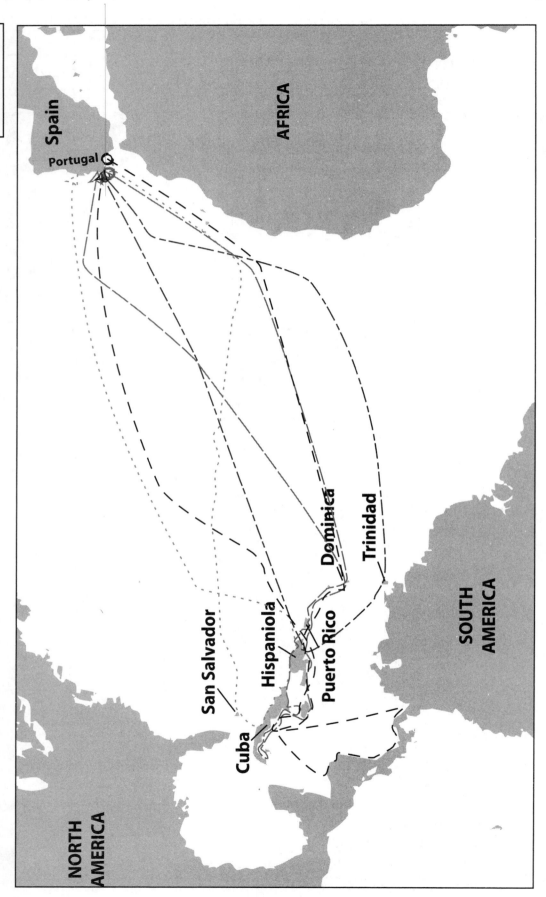

- - - - First Voyage (1492–1493)
———— Second Voyage (1493–1496)
– – – Third Voyage (1498–1500)
— – — Fourth Voyage (1502–1504)

Name: _____

Date: _____

The Four Voyages of Columbus: First Voyage

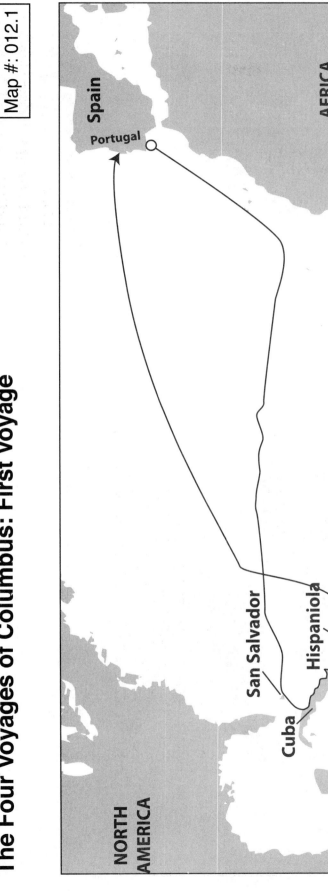

First Voyage (1492–1493)

Name: _____

Date: _____

The Four Voyages of Columbus: Second Voyage

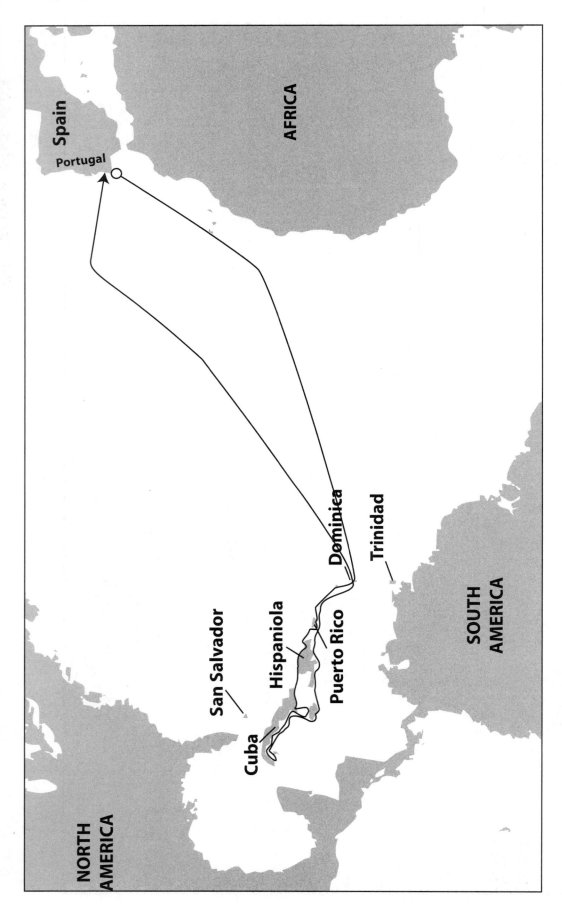

Second Voyage (1493–1496)

Spain

Portugal

AFRICA

Dominica

Trinidad

SOUTH AMERICA

San Salvador

Hispaniola

Puerto Rico

Cuba

NORTH AMERICA

Name: _____

Date: _____

The Four Voyages of Columbus: Third Voyage

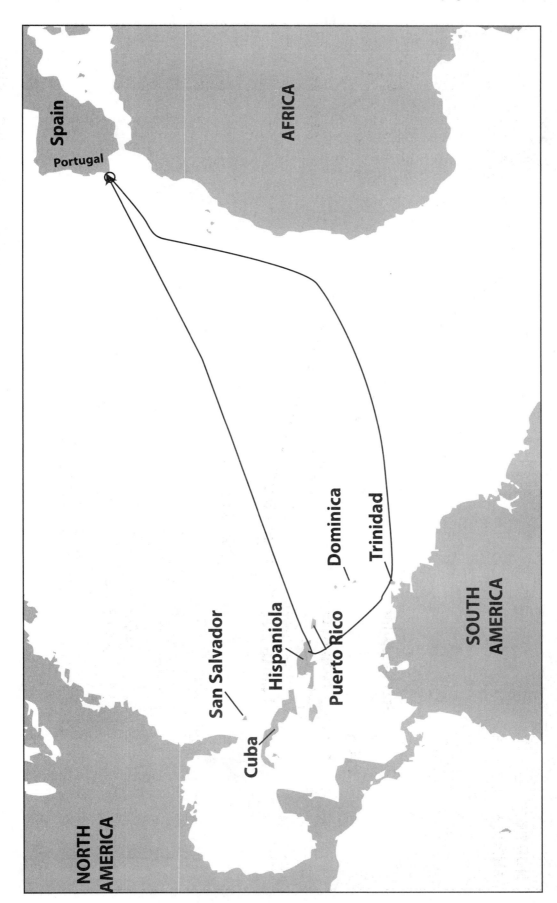

Third Voyage (1498–1500)

Name: _____

Date: _____

The Four Voyages of Columbus: Fourth Voyage

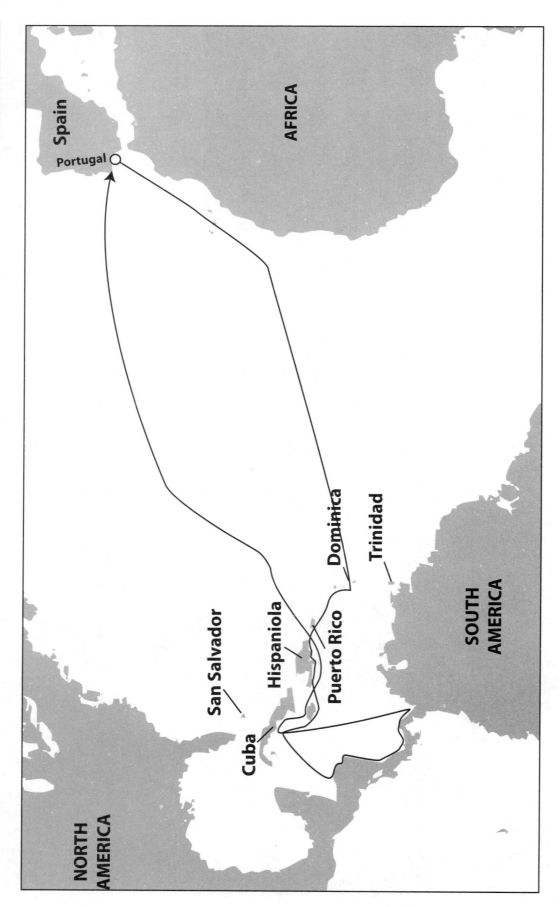

Fourth Voyage (1502–1504)

Spain

Portugal

AFRICA

Dominica

Trinidad

SOUTH AMERICA

San Salvador

Hispaniola

Puerto Rico

Cuba

NORTH AMERICA

Name: _____

Date: _____

The Columbian Exchange

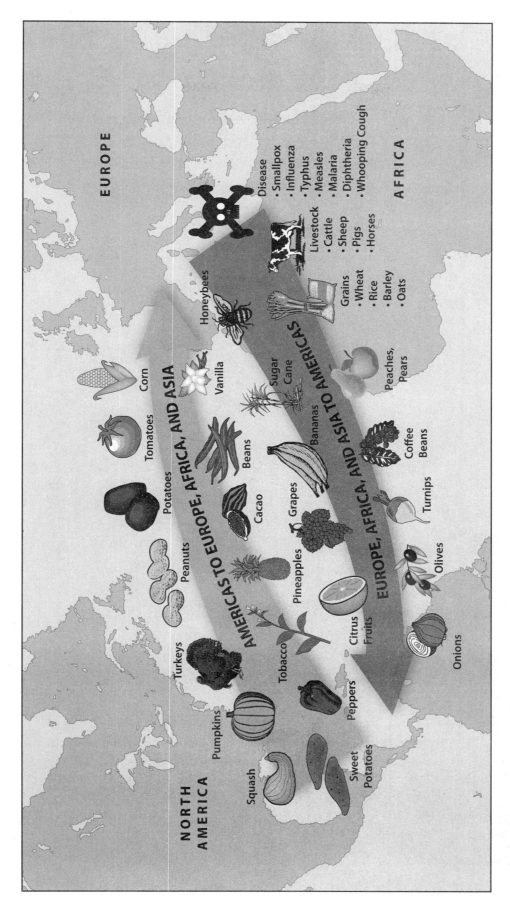

Name: _____

Date: _____

Spanish Exploration in the New World

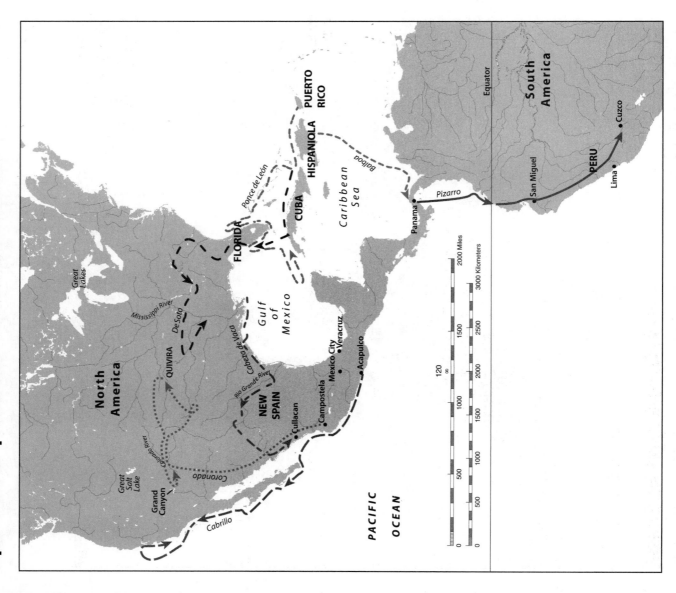

Name: _____

Date: _____

Voyages of Discovery

Map #: 015

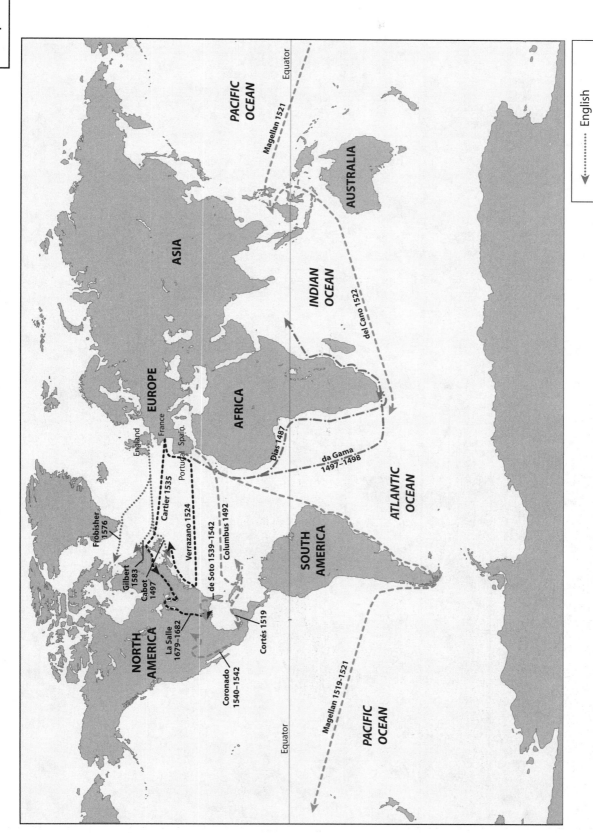

Name: _____

Date: _____

Magellan's Voyage Around the World

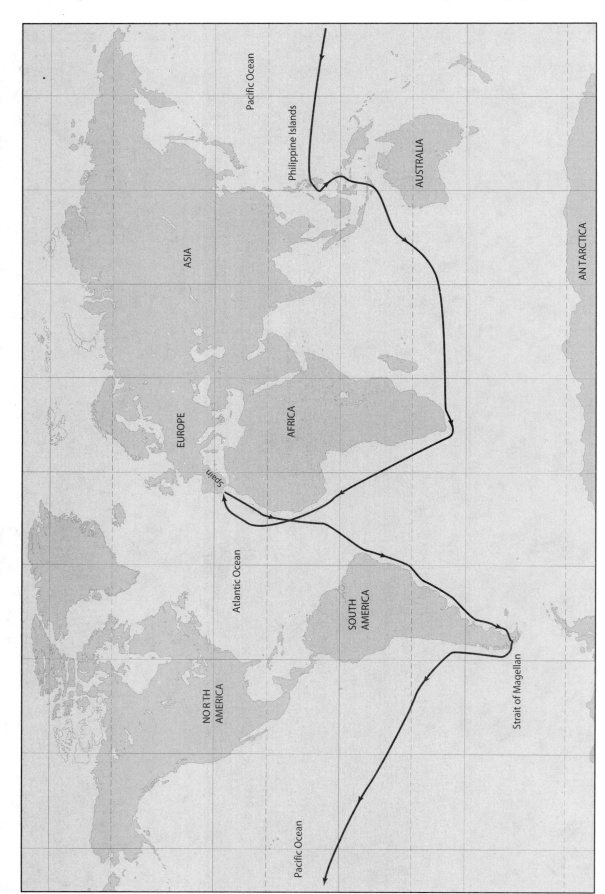

Name: _____

Date: _____

Early Explorers of North America

Map #: 017

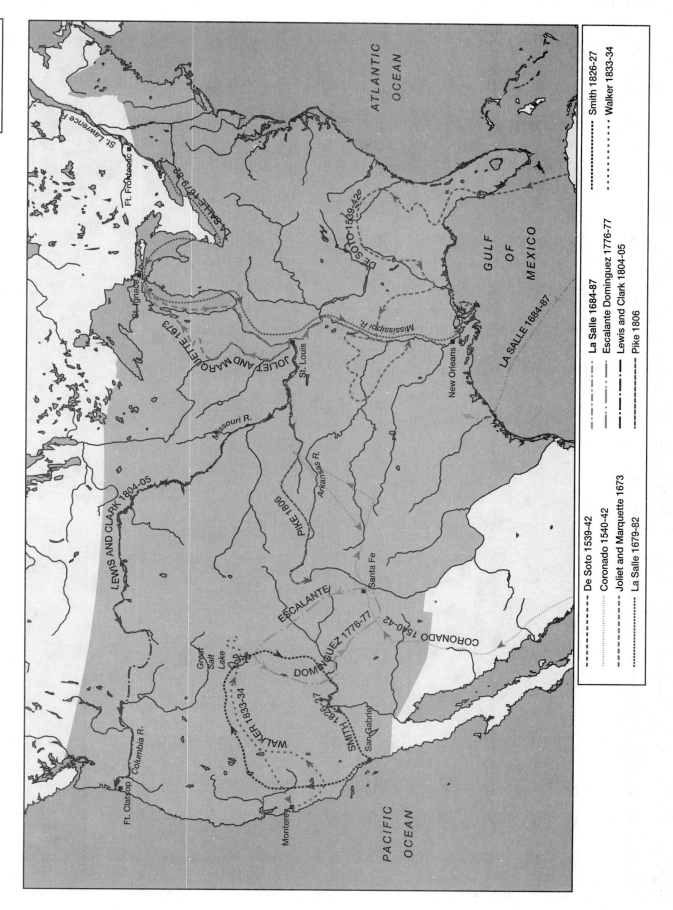

Legend:

- De Soto 1539-42
- Coronado 1540-42
- Joliet and Marquette 1673
- La Salle 1679-82
- La Salle 1684-87
- Escalante Domínguez 1776-77
- Lewis and Clark 1804-05
- Pike 1806
- Smith 1826-27
- Walker 1833-34

Name: _____

Date: _____

Early Explorers of North America With Modern State Borders

Map #: 017.1

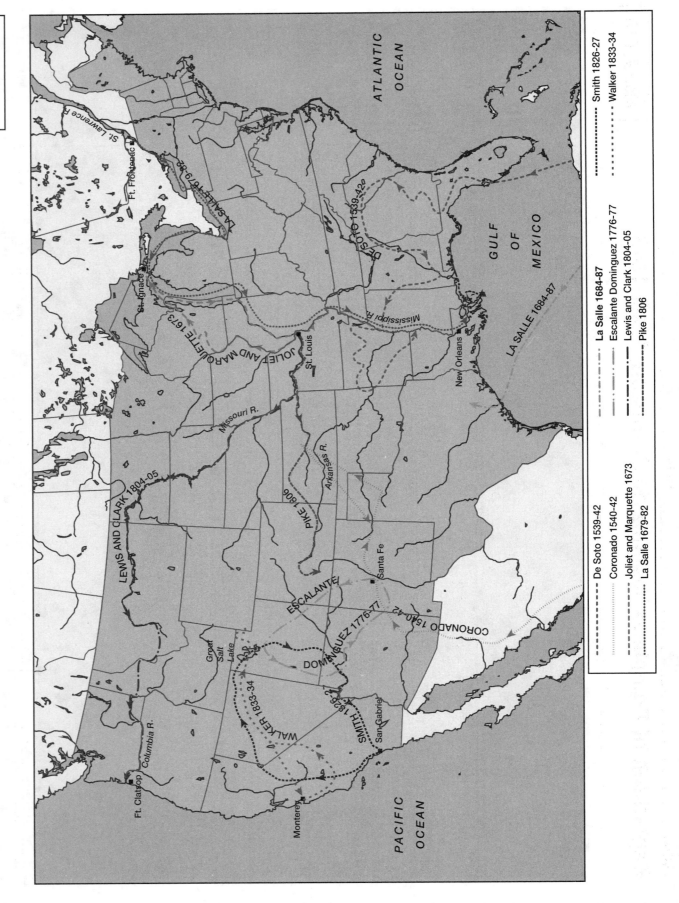

De Soto 1539-42 ....

Coronado 1540-42 ....

Joliet and Marquette 1673 ......

La Salle 1679-82 ....

La Salle 1684-87 ....

Escalante Dominguez 1776-77 ....

Lewis and Clark 1804-05 ....

Pike 1806 ....

Smith 1826-27 ....

Walker 1833-34 ....

Name: _____

Date: _____

Expedition of Francisco Vasquez de Coronado, 1540–1542

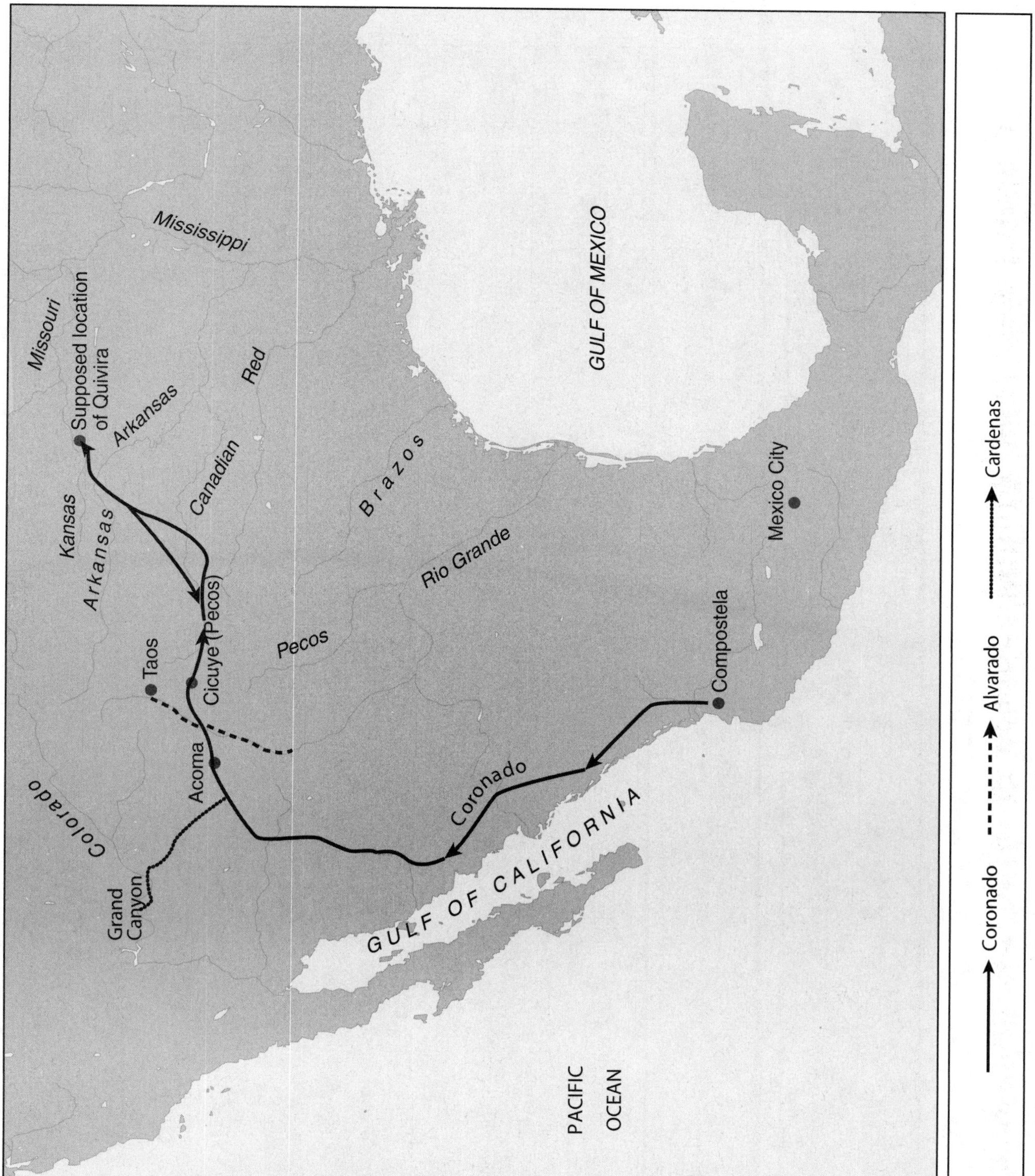

Map #: 018

Mississippi

Missouri

Supposed location of Quivira

Arkansas

Red

Kansas

Arkansas

Canadian

Brazos

Taos

Cicuye (Pecos)

Rio Grande

Pecos

Acoma

Colorado

Coronado

GULF OF CALIFORNIA

Grand Canyon

Compostela

Mexico City

GULF OF MEXICO

PACIFIC OCEAN

Coronado ———→

Alvarado ———→

Cardenas ———→

Name: _____   Date: _____

Expedition of Francisco Vasquez de Coronado, 1540–1542 With State Borders and Labels

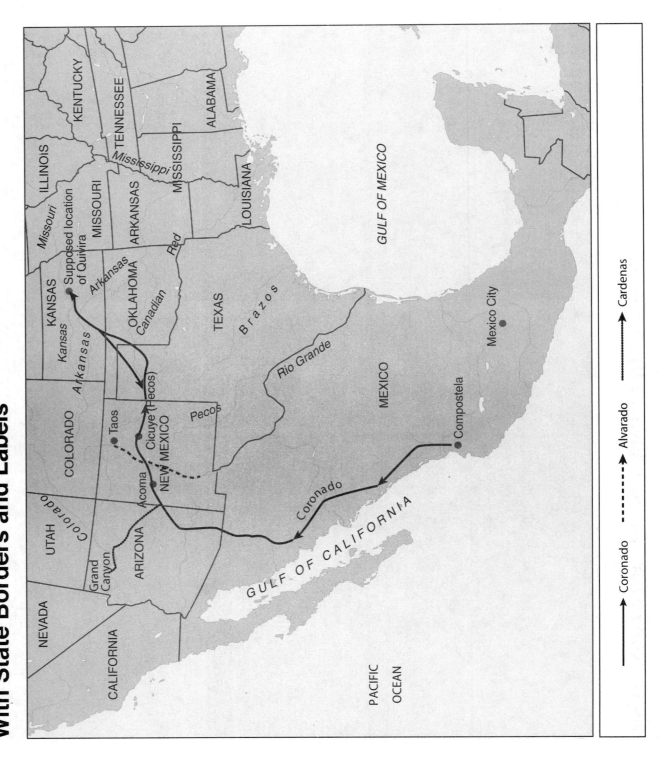

Name: _____

Date: _____

Major Native American Tribes in the 1600s

Atlantic Ocean

0   150   300 miles

0   150   300 kilometers

Micmac
Malecite
Abenaki
Pennacook
Massachusetts
Wampanoag
Narragansett
Mahican
Mohawk
Oneida
Iroquois
Onondaga
Cayuga
Seneca
Algonquin
Huron
Ottawa
Lenni-Lenape (Delaware)
Susquehannock
Powhatan
Tuscarora
Erie
Tutelo
Catawba
Shawnee
Cherokee
Yamasee
Timucua
Seminole
Calusa
Apalachee
Creek
Choctaw
Biloxi
Chickasaw
Quapaw
Caddo
Natchez
Atakapa
Karankawa

Hudson Bay

Chippewa (Ojibway)
Chippewa (Ojibway)
Menominee
Sauk
Fox
Winnebago
Kickapoo
Potawatomi
Miami
Illinois
Missouri
Osage
Wichita
Tonkawa

Assiniboin
Mandan
Hidatsa
Arikara
Sioux
Cheyenne
Ponca
Omaha Iowa
Pawnee
Kansa
Kiowa
Comanche
Arapaho
Kiowa

Okanagan
Kutenai
Colville
Spokane Gros Ventre
Blackfoot
Yakima
Nez Perce
Flathead
Cayuse
Bannock
Shoshone
Goshute
Ute
Southern Piute
Navajo
Hopi Pueblo
Zuni
Jicarilla Apache
Mescalero Apache
Lipan Apache
Concho
Tarahumara
Cahita
Yaqui

Makah
Quinault
Chehalis
Chinook
Tillamook
Umpqua
Yurok
Klamath
Modoc
Shasta
Hupa Maidu
Pomo
Miwok
Costanoan
Yokuts
Chumash
Serrano
Cahuilla
Mohave
Yavapi
Yuma
Pima
Maricopa
Papago
Western Apache
Opata
Seri
Concho
Cochimi
Cahita

Pacific Ocean

N E S W

Name: _____

Date: _____

Native Settlements and Trails in New England, 1600–1650

Map #: 020

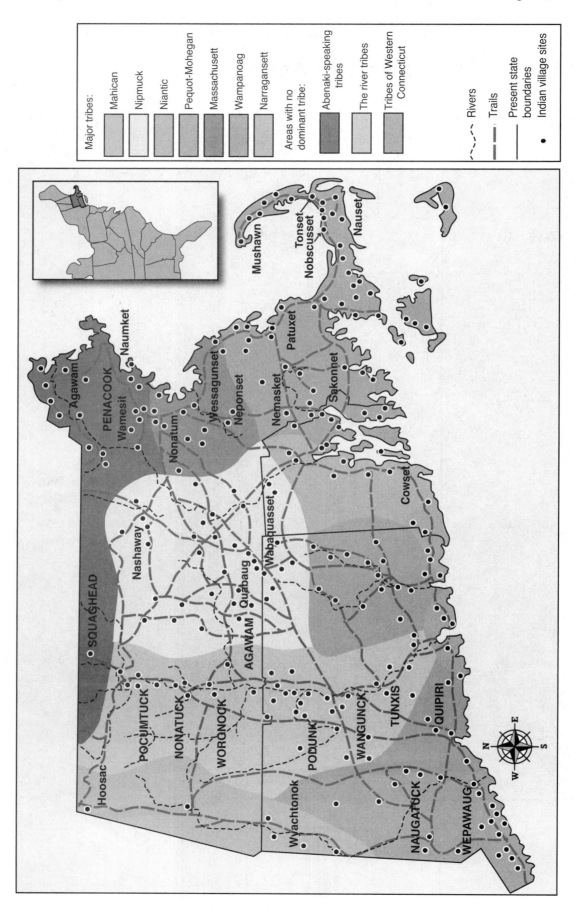

Major tribes:

Mahican

Nipmuck

Niantic

Pequot-Mohegan

Massachusett

Wampanoag

Narragansett

Areas with no dominant tribe:

Abenaki-speaking tribes

The river tribes

Tribes of Western Connecticut

- - - Rivers

Trails

Present state boundaries

• Indian village sites

Name: _____   Date: _____

First British Settlements in America

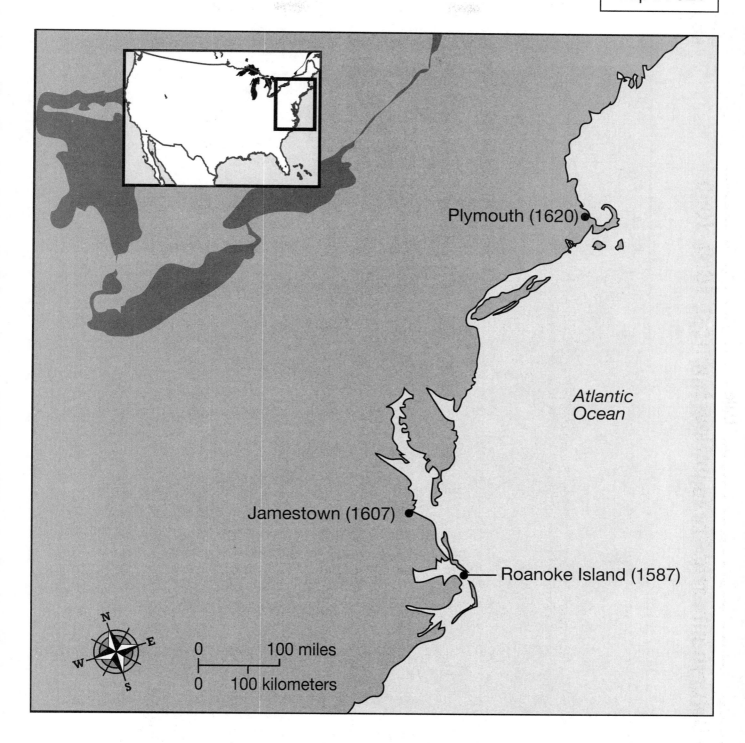

Plymouth (1620)

Atlantic Ocean

Jamestown (1607)

Roanoke Island (1587)

N E W S

0   100 miles

0   100 kilometers

Name: _____

Date: _____

Slave Trade From Africa to the Americas, 1650 to 1860

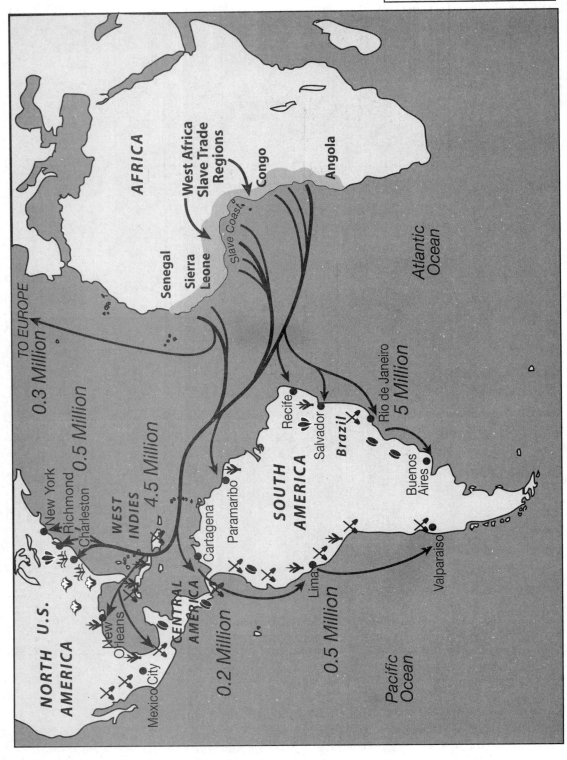

Legend:
- Tobacco
- Coffee
- Cotton
- Sugar
- Mining
- Rice
- Major Slave Trade Route

AFRICA

West Africa Slave Trade Regions

Senegal

Sierra Leone

Slave Coast

Congo

Angola

Atlantic Ocean

TO EUROPE

0.3 Million

0.5 Million

4.5 Million

NORTH AMERICA

U.S.

New York

Richmond

Charleston

WEST INDIES

New Orleans

Mexico City

CENTRAL AMERICA

0.2 Million

Cartagena

Paramaribo

SOUTH AMERICA

Recife

Salvador

Brazil

Rio de Janeiro

5 Million

Buenos Aires

Lima

0.5 Million

Valparaiso

Pacific Ocean

Name: _____   Date: _____

Triangular Trade

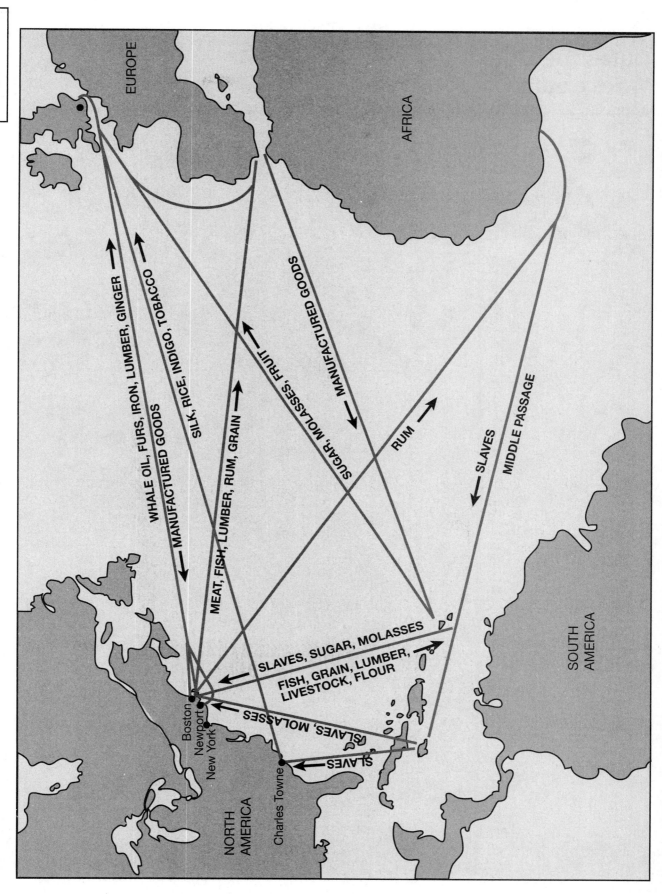

Name: _____   Date: _____

Dates the British Colonies in America Were Settled

Map #: 024

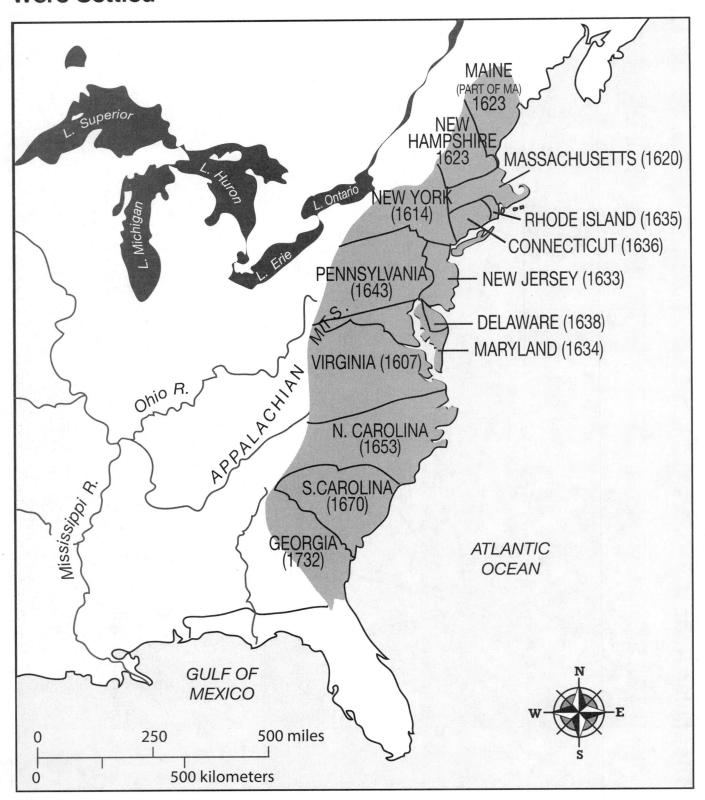

L. Superior

L. Huron

L. Michigan

L. Ontario

L. Erie

MAINE
(PART OF MA)
1623

NEW
HAMPSHIRE
1623

MASSACHUSETTS (1620)

NEW YORK
(1614)

RHODE ISLAND (1635)

CONNECTICUT (1636)

PENNSYLVANIA
(1643)

NEW JERSEY (1633)

DELAWARE (1638)

MARYLAND (1634)

VIRGINIA (1607)

N. CAROLINA
(1653)

S. CAROLINA
(1670)

GEORGIA
(1732)

ATLANTIC
OCEAN

APPALACHIAN MTS.

Ohio R.

Mississippi R.

GULF OF
MEXICO

N
W   E
S

0   250   500 miles

0   500 kilometers

Name: _____ Date: _____

The Thirteen British Colonies in America

Map #: 025

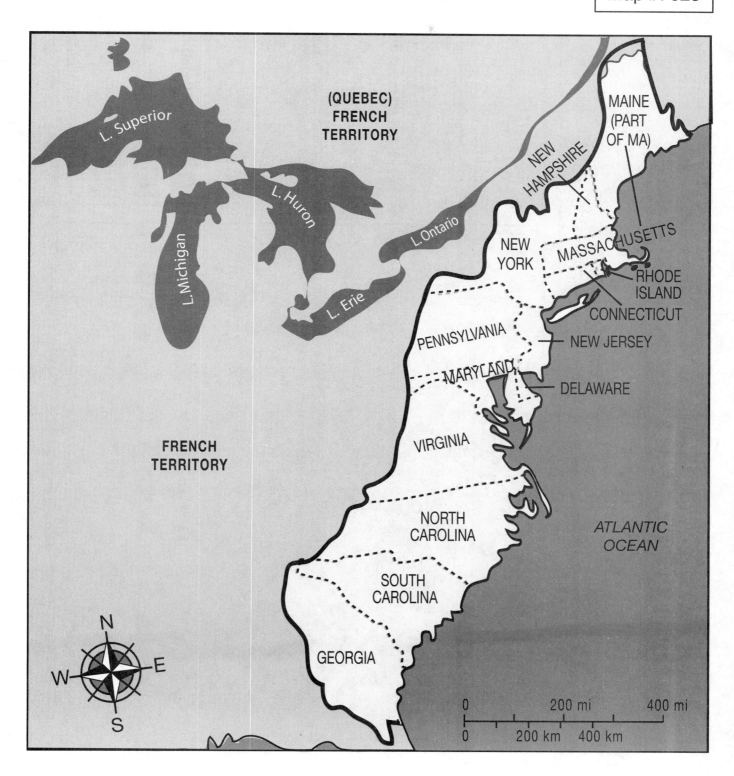

Name: _____

Date: _____

The New England, Middle, and Southern Colonies

Map #: 026

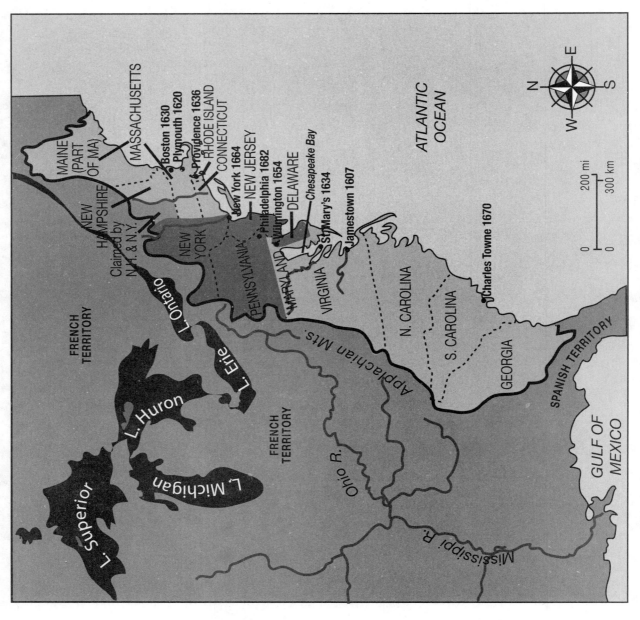

Legend:
- New England colonies
- Middle colonies
- Southern colonies
- Proclamation Line of 1763

MAINE (PART OF MA)

NEW HAMPSHIRE

Claimed by N.H. & N.Y.

MASSACHUSETTS

Boston 1630
Plymouth 1620
Providence 1636
RHODE ISLAND
CONNECTICUT

NEW YORK

NEW JERSEY

New York 1664
Philadelphia 1682
Wilmington 1654
DELAWARE

PENNSYLVANIA

MARYLAND

St. Mary's 1634

Chesapeake Bay

Jamestown 1607

VIRGINIA

N. CAROLINA

S. CAROLINA

Charles Towne 1670

GEORGIA

SPANISH TERRITORY

GULF OF MEXICO

ATLANTIC OCEAN

Appalachian Mts.

Ohio R.

FRENCH TERRITORY

Mississippi R.

L. Superior

L. Michigan

L. Huron

L. Erie

L. Ontario

FRENCH TERRITORY

200 mi
300 km

Name: _____   Date: _____

The New England Colonies

Map #: 027

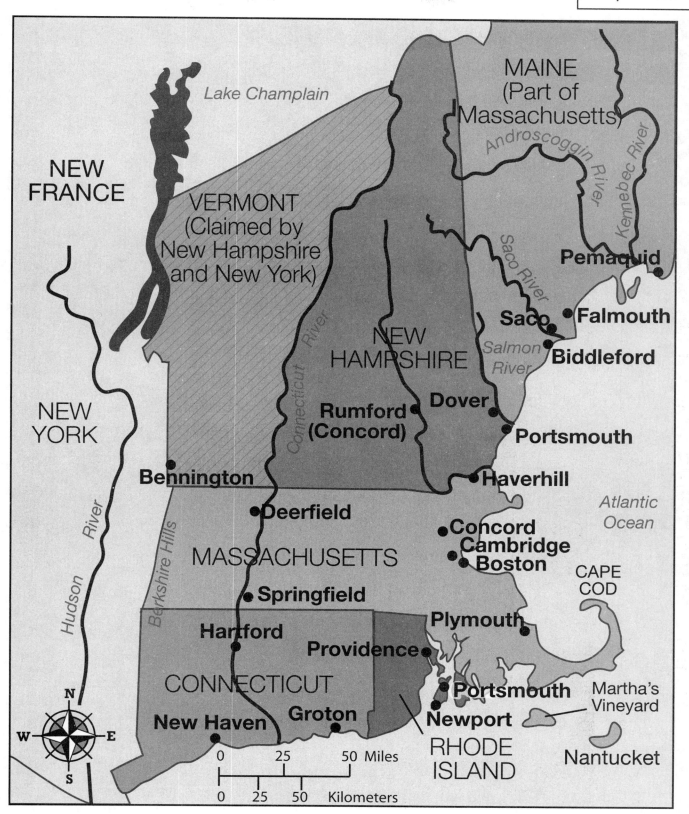

Name: _____   Date: _____

The Middle Colonies

Map #: 028

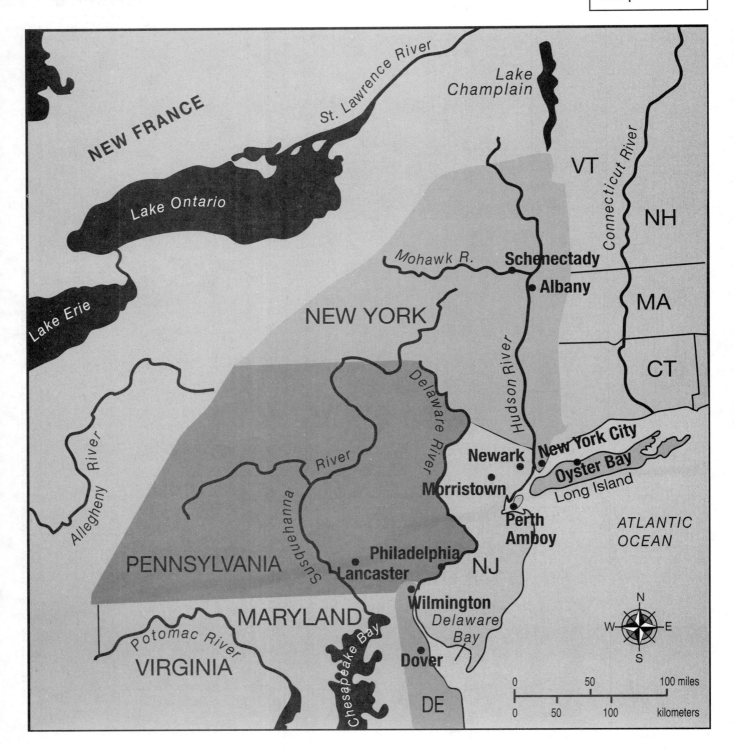

Name: _____ Date: _____

The Southern Colonies

Map #: 029

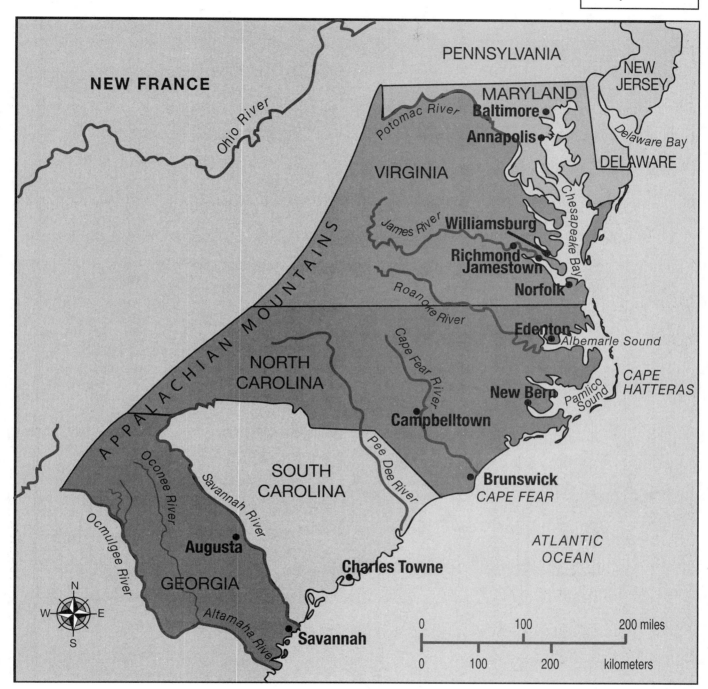

Name: _____ Date: _____

Settlement Patterns of European Immigrants in the Thirteen Colonies

Map #: 030

Legend:
- English
- German
- Scots-Irish
- Scotish
- Dutch
- Proclamation Line of 1763

Name: _____ Date: _____

Economics of the British Colonies

Map #: 031

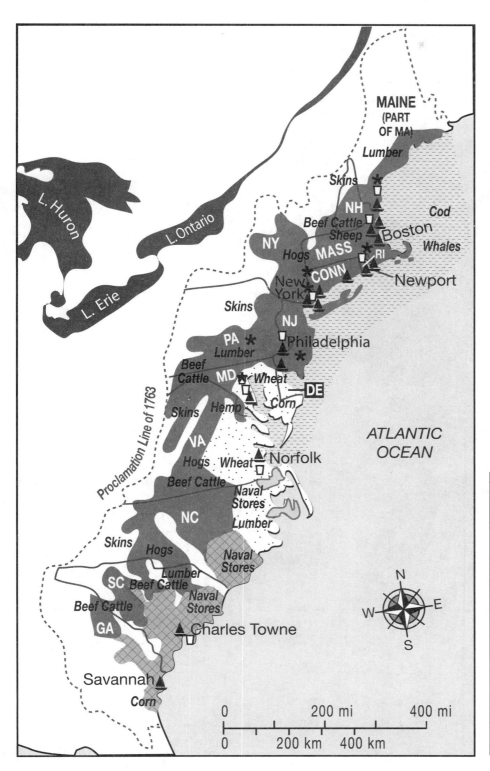

MAINE
(PART OF MA)

Lumber

Skins

NH

Beef Cattle
Sheep

Cod

Boston

Whales

NY

Hogs

MASS

CONN

RI

Newport

New York

Skins

NJ

PA

Philadelphia

Lumber

Beef Cattle

MD

Wheat

DE

Corn

Skins

Hemp

VA

Hogs

Wheat

Norfolk

Beef Cattle

Naval Stores

NC

Lumber

Skins

Hogs

Lumber

Naval Stores

SC

Beef Cattle

Naval Stores

Beef Cattle

GA

Charles Towne

Savannah

Corn

L. Huron

L. Ontario

L. Erie

Proclamation Line of 1763

ATLANTIC OCEAN

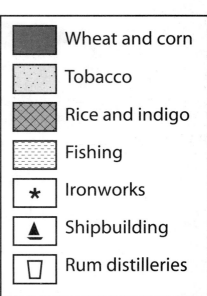

Wheat and corn

Tobacco

Rice and indigo

Fishing

* Ironworks

▲ Shipbuilding

Rum distilleries

0   200 mi   400 mi

0   200 km   400 km

N
W   E
S

Name: _____   Date: _____

European Colonial Territories in Eastern North America Prior to 1763

Map #: 032

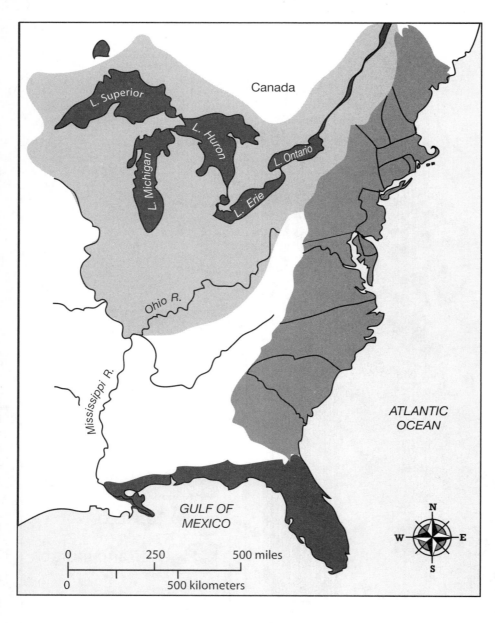

Canada

L. Superior

L. Huron

L. Michigan

L. Ontario

L. Erie

Ohio R.

Mississippi R.

ATLANTIC
OCEAN

GULF OF
MEXICO

| 0 | 250 | 500 miles |

| 0 | 500 kilometers |

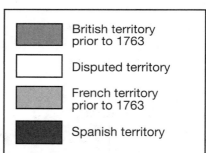

British territory
prior to 1763

Disputed territory

French territory
prior to 1763

Spanish territory

Name: _____ Date: _____

French Forts in French Territory in North America

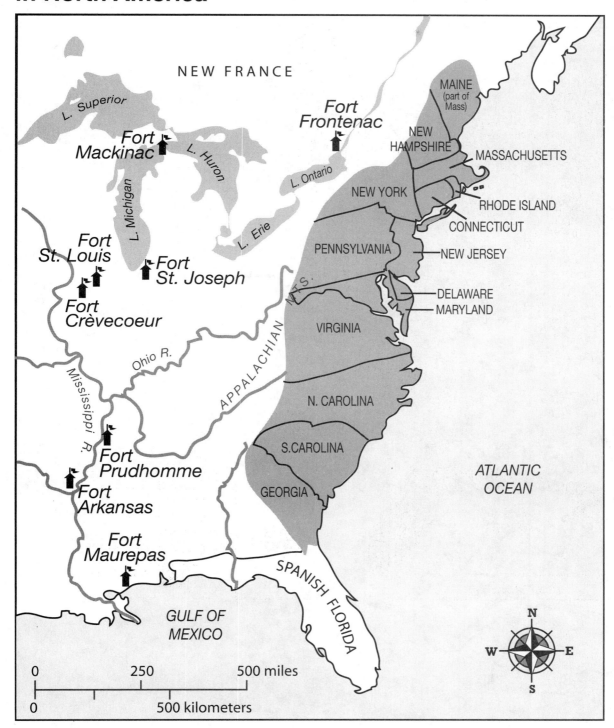

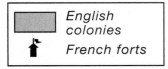
English colonies
French forts

Name: _____

Date: _____

French, Spanish, and English Land Claims
Prior to the French and Indian War

Legend:
- Land claimed by France, 1750
- Land claimed by Spain, 1750
- Land claimed by England, 1750

ATLANTIC OCEAN

GULF OF MEXICO

CANADA

MEXICO

PACIFIC OCEAN

200 mi

300 km

0

0

N E S W

Name: _____

Date: _____

Land Taken From Native Americans, Before 1750–1810

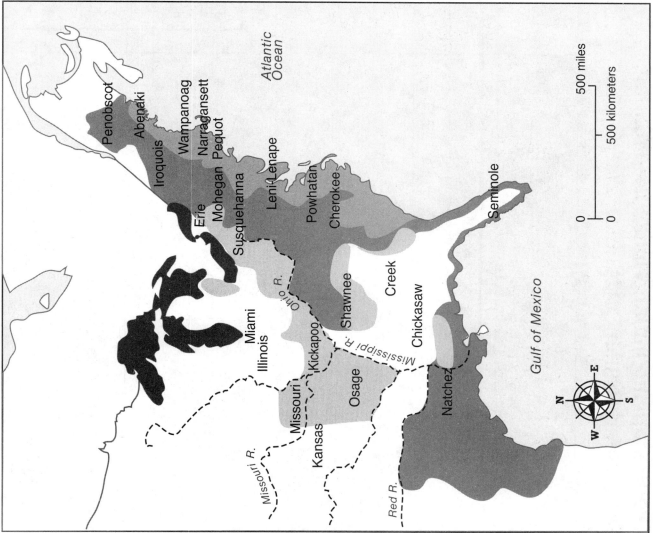

Land taken before 1750

Land taken 1750-1783

Land taken 1784-1810

Penobscot

Abenaki

Iroquois

Wampanoag

Narragansett

Mohegan Pequot

Erie

Susquehanna

Leni Lenape

Powhatan

Cherokee

Seminole

Atlantic Ocean

Shawnee

Creek

Chickasaw

Miami

Illinois

Kickapoo

Osage

Natchez

Missouri

Kansas

Ohio R.

Mississippi R.

Missouri R.

Red R.

Gulf of Mexico

N E S W

500 miles

500 kilometers

0

Name: _____

Date: _____

The French and Indian War, 1754–1763: French and British Forts

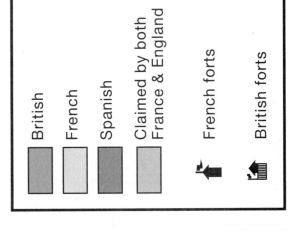

British

French

Spanish

Claimed by both France & England

French forts

British forts

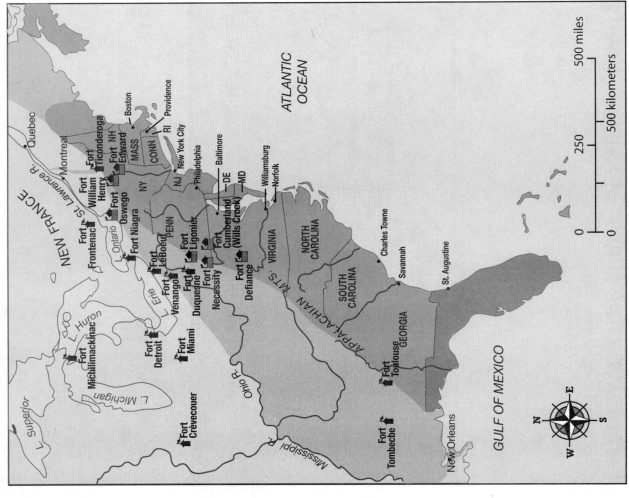

Name: _____

Date: _____

Map #: 037

Territorial Claims in the French and Indian War, 1754–1763

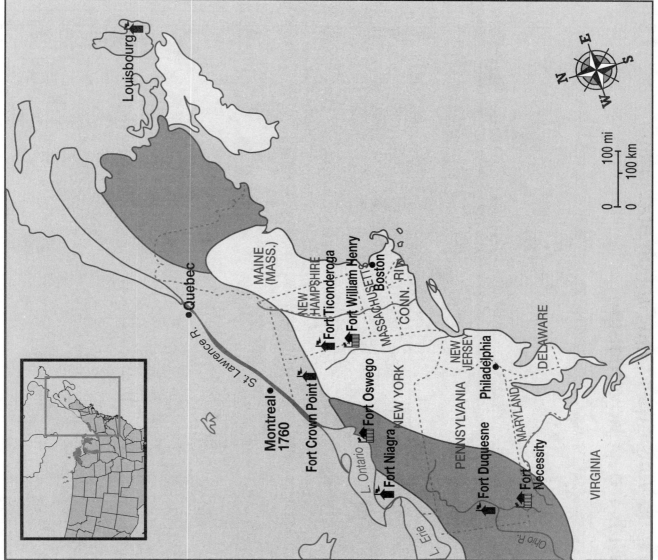

Louisbourg

Quebec

Montreal
1760

St. Lawrence R.

Fort Crown Point

Fort Ticonderoga

Fort William Henry

MAINE
(MASS.)

NEW
HAMPSHIRE

MASSACHUSETTS

Boston

CONN.

R.I.

Fort Oswego

Fort Niagra

L. Ontario

NEW YORK

NEW
JERSEY

Philadelphia

PENNSYLVANIA

Fort Duquesne

MARYLAND

DELAWARE

Fort
Necessity

VIRGINIA

Ohio R.

L. Erie

British territory

French territory

Disputed territory

French forts

British forts

100 mi

100 km

0

0

Name: _____

Date: _____

Map #: 037.1

Battle Victories of the French and Indian War, 1754–1763 With Troop Movements

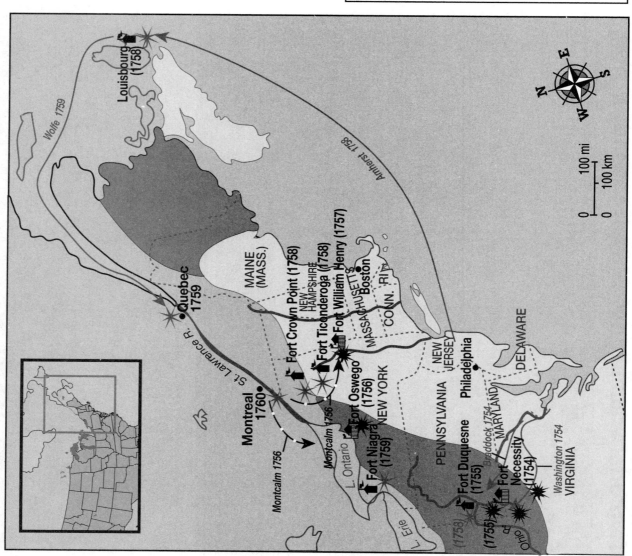

Legend:
- British territory
- French territory
- Disputed territory
- British forts
- French forts
- British victories
- French victories
- British forces
- French forces

Louisbourg (1758)

Wolfe 1759

Amherst 1758

Quebec 1759

St. Lawrence R.

Montreal 1760

Montcalm 1756

MAINE (MASS.)

NEW HAMPSHIRE

Fort Crown Point (1758)

Fort Ticonderoga (1758)

Fort William Henry (1757)

Boston

MASSACHUSETTS

CONN.   R.I.

Fort Oswego (1756)

NEW YORK

NEW JERSEY

Philadelphia

PENNSYLVANIA

DELAWARE

Fort Niagara (1759)

L. Ontario

L. Erie

Fort Duquesne (1755)

Braddock 1754

MARYLAND

Fort Necessity (1754)

Washington 1754

VIRGINIA

(1758)

(1755)

Ohio R.

Name: _____ Date: _____

The Proclamation Line of 1763

Map #: 038

Name: _____

Date: _____

Treaty of Paris, 1763

Map #: 039

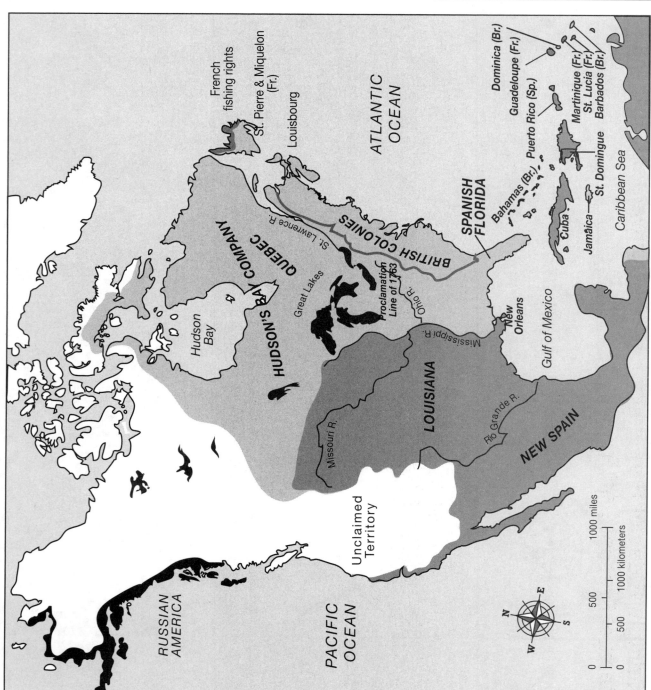

Legend:
- British
- Spanish
- French
- Russian
- Unclaimed Territory
- Proclamation Line of 1763

French fishing rights
St. Pierre & Miquelon (Fr.)
Louisbourg
ATLANTIC OCEAN
St. Lawrence R.
QUEBEC
HUDSON'S BAY COMPANY
Hudson Bay
Great Lakes
Proclamation Line of 1763
Ohio R.
BRITISH COLONIES
SPANISH FLORIDA
Dominica (Br.)
Guadeloupe (Fr.)
Puerto Rico (Sp.)
Martinique (Fr.)
St. Lucia (Fr.)
Barbados (Br.)
Bahamas (Br.)
Cuba
Jamaica
St. Domingue
Caribbean Sea
New Orleans
Gulf of Mexico
Mississippi R.
LOUISIANA
Missouri R.
Rio Grande R.
NEW SPAIN
Unclaimed Territory
PACIFIC OCEAN
RUSSIAN AMERICA

1000 miles
1000 kilometers
500
500
0
0

N E S W

Name:

Date:

Midnight Rides of Paul Revere, William Dawes, and Samuel Prescott: All Routes

Map #: 040

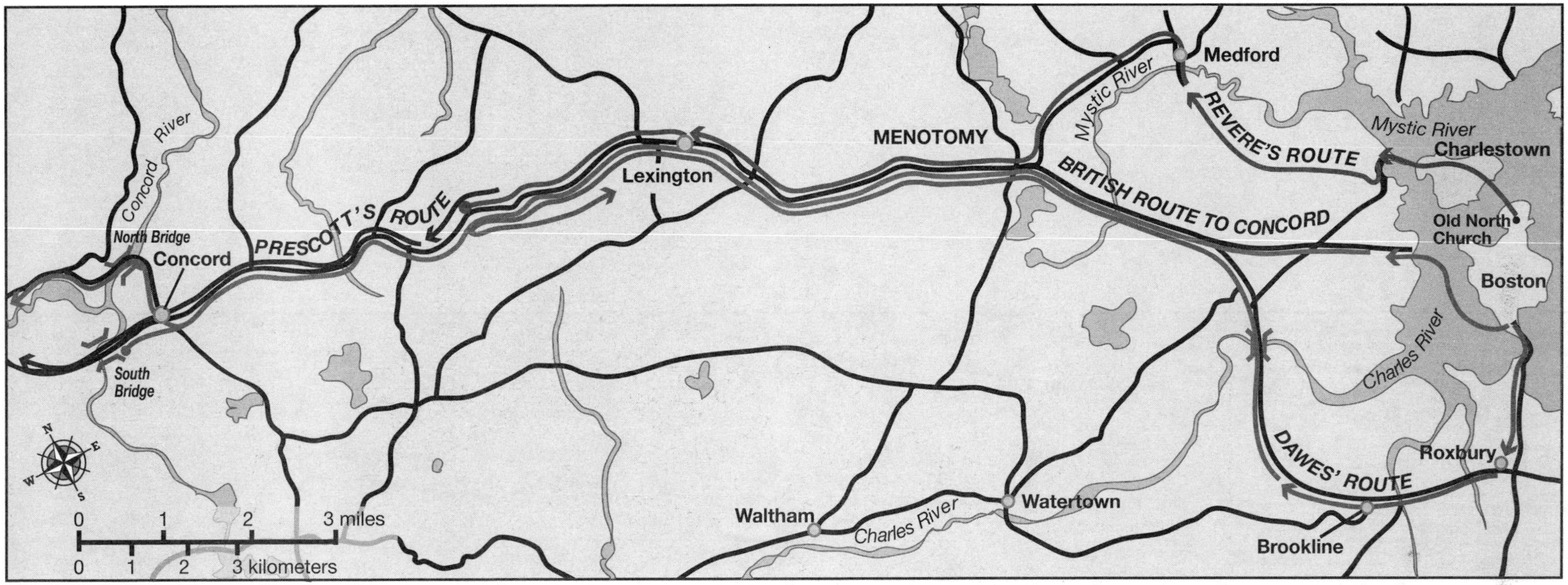

Name: _____

Date: _____

Midnight Rides of Paul Revere, William Dawes, and Samuel Prescott: Paul Revere's Route

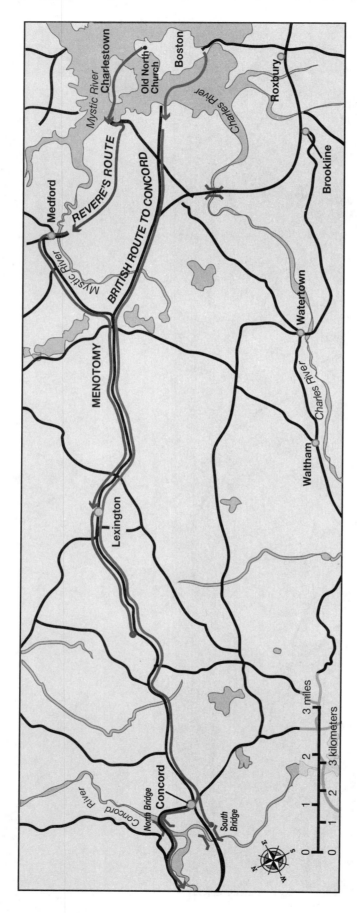

Name: _____

Date: _____

Midnight Rides of Paul Revere, William Dawes, and Samuel Prescott: William Dawes' Route

Map #: 040.2

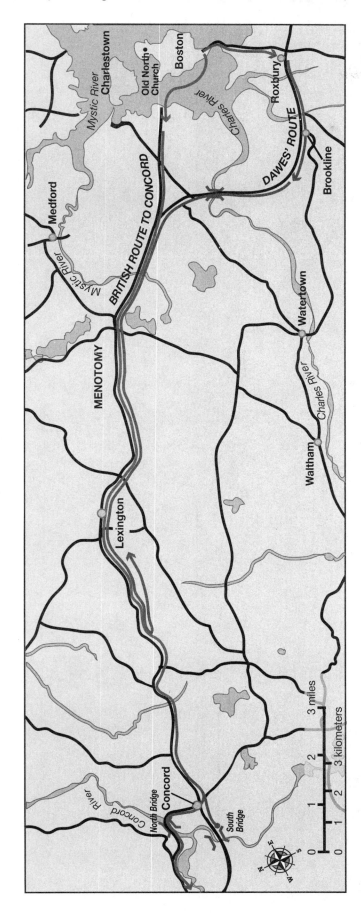

Name: _____

Date: _____

Midnight Rides of Paul Revere, William Dawes, and Samuel Prescott: Samuel Prescott's Route

Map #: 040.3

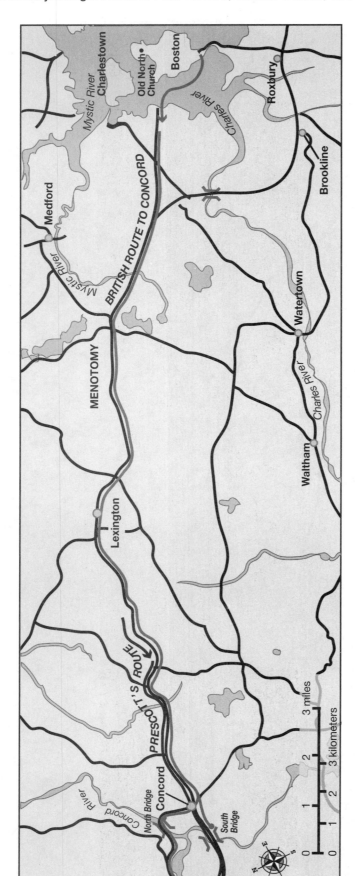

Name: _____

Date: _____

Battles of Lexington and Concord, April 18–19, 1775

Map #: 041

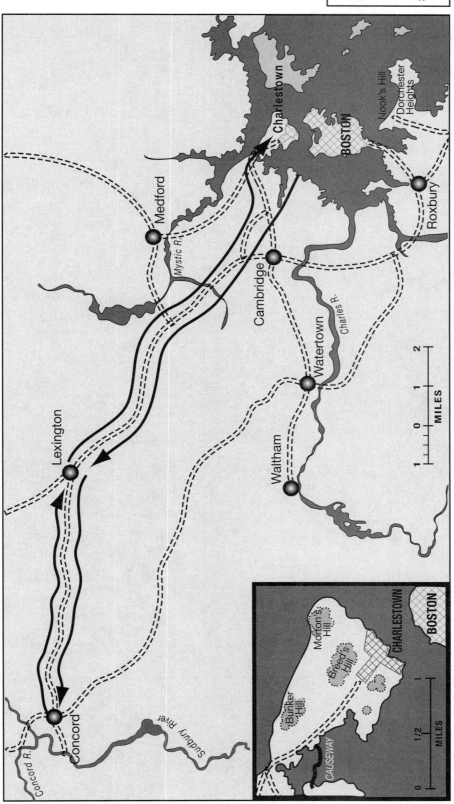

Route of British troops

Roads

CHARLESTOWN

BOSTON

Charlestown

Medford

Mystic R.

Cambridge

Watertown

Charles R.

Roxbury

Nook's Hill

Dorchester Heights

BOSTON

Waltham

Lexington

Concord

Concord R.

Sudbury River

MILES

2   1   0   1

Morton's Hill

Breed's Hill

Bunker Hill

CHARLESTOWN

BOSTON

CAUSEWAY

MILES

1   1/2   0

Name: _____ Date: _____

Battles of the American Revolution

Map #: 042

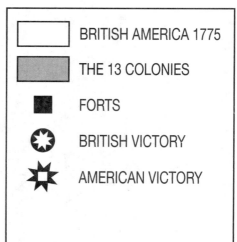

	BRITISH AMERICA 1775
	THE 13 COLONIES
	FORTS
	BRITISH VICTORY
	AMERICAN VICTORY

Name: _____

Date: _____

Treaty of Paris, 1783

Map #: 043

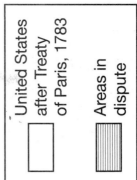

United States after Treaty of Paris, 1783

Areas in dispute

British Territory

Spanish Territory

Name: _____

Date: _____

Western Land Claims Ceded by the States, 1782–1802

Map #: 044

	Boundary of territory ceded by New York
	Boundary of territory ceded by Virginia
	Original thirteen states after their land cession

BRITISH NORTH AMERICA (CANADA)

LOWER CANADA

UPPER CANADA

St. Lawrence R.

Lake Superior

Lake Huron

Lake Michigan

Lake Ontario

Lake Erie

VERMONT

NEW HAMPSHIRE

MAINE (part of Mass.)

MASSACHUSETTS

RHODE ISLAND

CONNECTICUT

NEW YORK

NEW JERSEY

PENNSYLVANIA

DELAWARE

MARYLAND

D.C.

VIRGINIA

NORTH CAROLINA

SOUTH CAROLINA

GEORGIA

ATLANTIC OCEAN

SPANISH FLORIDA

Gulf of Mexico

NORTHWEST TERRITORY Ceded by Virginia 1784

Ceded by Massachusetts 1785

Ceded by Connecticut 1786

Ceded by Connecticut 1800

Ceded by New York 1782

Ohio R.

Missouri R.

Mississippi R.

Territory of Virginia until 1792 (Kentucky)

Ceded by New York 1782

Cumberland Gap

State of Franklin

Ceded by N. Carolina 1790 (Tennessee)

Ceded by South Carolina to Georgia 1787

Ceded by Georgia 1802

Ceded by Spain 1795

31° North Latitude

400 miles

400 kilometers

200

200

0

0

Name: _____

Date: _____

Territorial Acquisitions, 1783–1853

Map #: 045

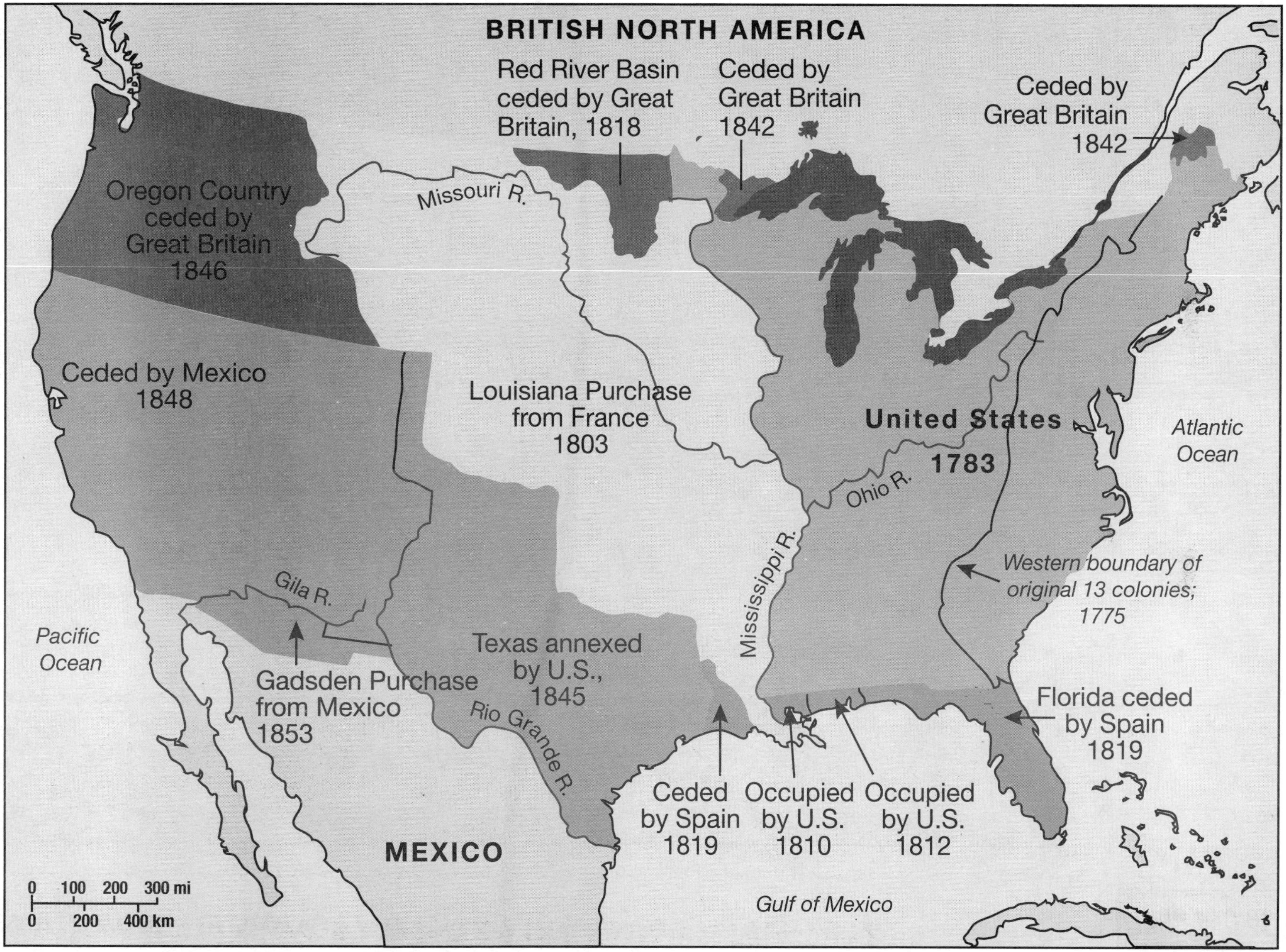

BRITISH NORTH AMERICA

Ceded by Great Britain 1842

Ceded by Great Britain 1842

Red River Basin ceded by Great Britain, 1818

Missouri R.

Oregon Country ceded by Great Britain 1846

Louisiana Purchase from France 1803

Ceded by Mexico 1848

Gila R.

Texas annexed by U.S., 1845

Gadsden Purchase from Mexico 1853

Rio Grande R.

MEXICO

United States 1783

Ohio R.

Mississippi R.

Western boundary of original 13 colonies; 1775

Florida ceded by Spain 1819

Occupied by U.S. 1812

Occupied by U.S. 1810

Ceded by Spain 1819

Atlantic Ocean

Gulf of Mexico

Pacific Ocean

0   100   200   300 mi

0   200   400 km

Name: _____

Date: _____

Northwest Territory, 1787

Map #: 046

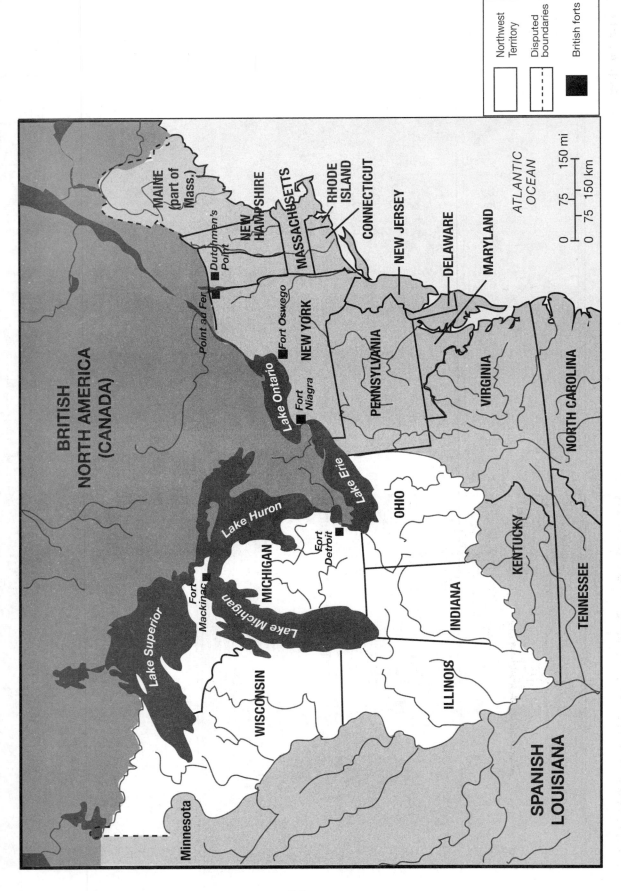

Northwest Territory

Disputed boundaries

British forts

Name: _____

Date: _____

Ratification of the Constitution

Map #: 047

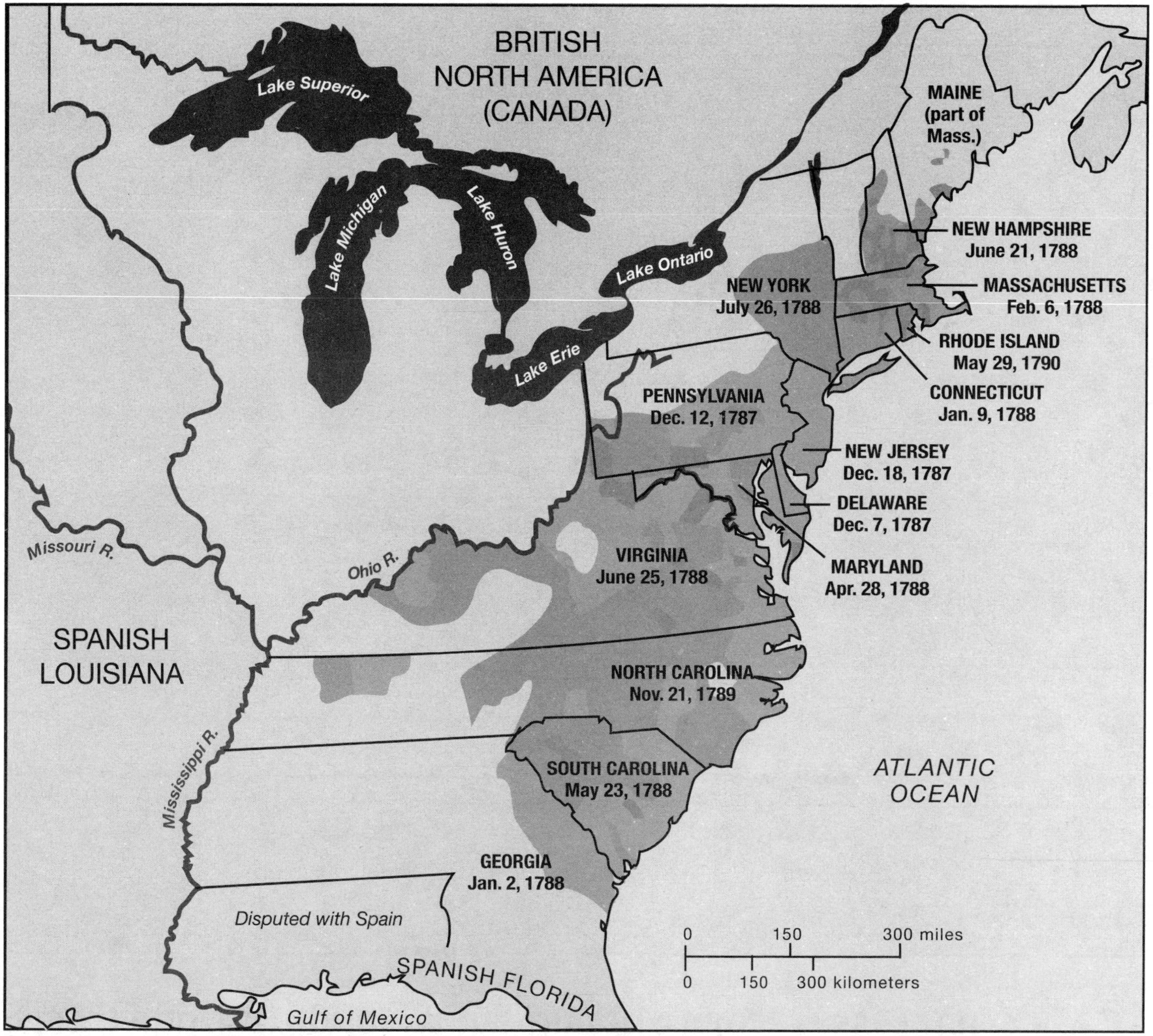

Legend:
- Majority for Ratification
- Majority against Ratification
- Divided
- No returns

BRITISH NORTH AMERICA (CANADA)

Lake Superior

Lake Michigan

Lake Huron

Lake Ontario

Lake Erie

MAINE (part of Mass.)

NEW HAMPSHIRE
June 21, 1788

MASSACHUSETTS
Feb. 6, 1788

RHODE ISLAND
May 29, 1790

CONNECTICUT
Jan. 9, 1788

NEW YORK
July 26, 1788

PENNSYLVANIA
Dec. 12, 1787

NEW JERSEY
Dec. 18, 1787

DELAWARE
Dec. 7, 1787

MARYLAND
Apr. 28, 1788

VIRGINIA
June 25, 1788

NORTH CAROLINA
Nov. 21, 1789

SOUTH CAROLINA
May 23, 1788

GEORGIA
Jan. 2, 1788

ATLANTIC OCEAN

SPANISH FLORIDA

Gulf of Mexico

Disputed with Spain

SPANISH LOUISIANA

Ohio R.

Mississippi R.

Missouri R.

300 miles

300 kilometers

150

150

0

0

Name: _____

Date: _____

States and Territories of the United States, 1789–1790

Map #: 048

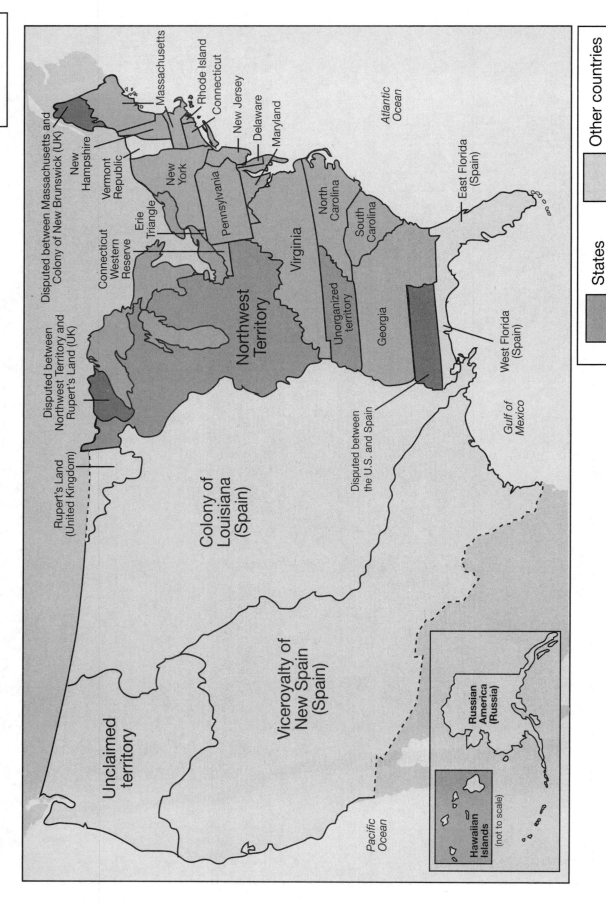

Massachusetts
Rhode Island
Connecticut
New Jersey
Delaware
Maryland
Disputed between Massachusetts and Colony of New Brunswick (UK)
New Hampshire
Vermont Republic
New York
Pennsylvania
Connecticut Western Reserve
Erie Triangle
Virginia
North Carolina
South Carolina
Atlantic Ocean
East Florida (Spain)
Northwest Territory
Unorganized territory
Georgia
West Florida (Spain)
Disputed between Northwest Territory and Rupert's Land (UK)
Rupert's Land (United Kingdom)
Colony of Louisiana (Spain)
Disputed between the U.S. and Spain
Gulf of Mexico
Unclaimed territory
Viceroyalty of New Spain (Spain)
Pacific Ocean
Russian America (Russia)
Hawaiian Islands (not to scale)

Other countries
Disputed areas
States
Territories

Name: _____

Date: _____

Pinckney's Treaty, 1795

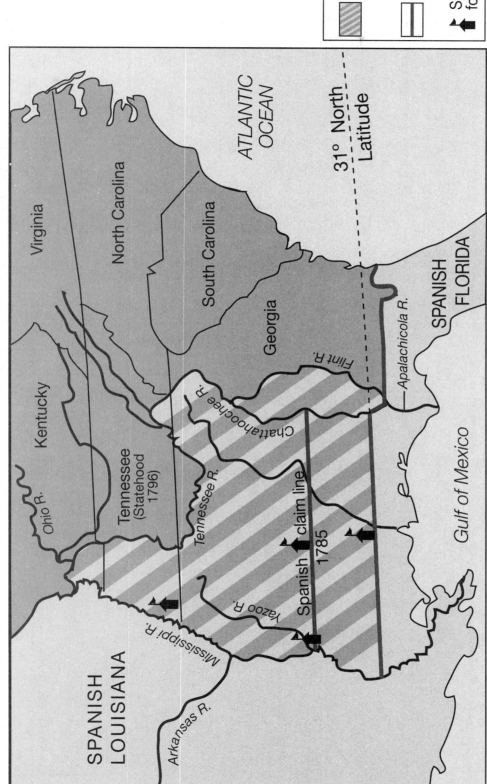

Legend:

- Maximum Spanish claim, 1784
- Line of Pinckney's Treaty
- Spanish-held forts

ATLANTIC OCEAN

31° North Latitude

Virginia

North Carolina

South Carolina

Georgia

SPANISH FLORIDA

Apalachicola R.

Flint R.

Chattahoochee R.

Kentucky

Tennessee (Statehood 1796)

Tennessee R.

Ohio R.

Spanish claim line 1785

Yazoo R.

Gulf of Mexico

SPANISH LOUISIANA

Mississippi R.

Arkansas R.

Map #: 050

Name: _____

Date: _____

Early Roads to the West

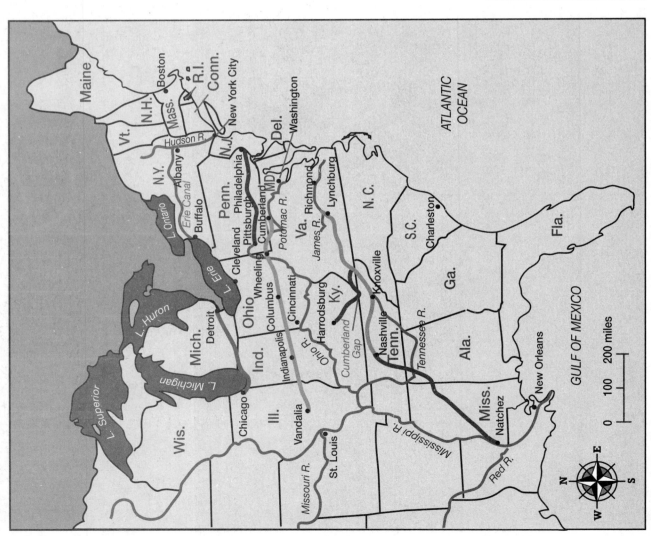

Legend:
- National Road
- Chicago Turnpike
- Pennsylvania Road
- Wilderness Road
- Great Valley Road
- Natchez Trace

Name: _____

Date: _____

States and Territories of the United States, 1802

Map #: 051

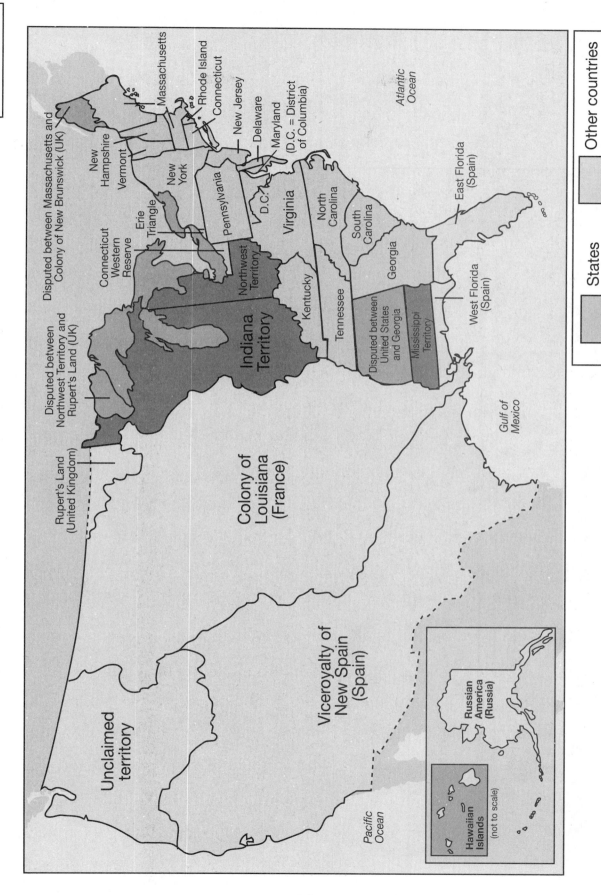

Atlantic Ocean

East Florida (Spain)

Gulf of Mexico

West Florida (Spain)

Massachusetts

Rhode Island

Connecticut

New Jersey

Delaware

Maryland

(D.C. = District of Columbia)

New Hampshire

Vermont

New York

Pennsylvania

D.C.

Virginia

North Carolina

South Carolina

Georgia

Disputed between Massachusetts and Colony of New Brunswick (UK)

Connecticut Western Reserve

Erie Triangle

Northwest Territory

Indiana Territory

Kentucky

Tennessee

Disputed between United States and Georgia

Mississippi Territory

Disputed between Northwest Territory and Rupert's Land (UK)

Rupert's Land (United Kingdom)

Colony of Louisiana (France)

Unclaimed territory

Viceroyalty of New Spain (Spain)

Pacific Ocean

Russian America (Russia)

Hawaiian Islands (not to scale)

Other countries | **Disputed areas** | **States** | **Territories**

CD-404247 ©Mark Twain Media, Inc., Publishers

Name: _____

Date: _____

Louisiana Purchase, 1803

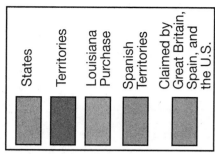

States

Territories

Louisiana Purchase

Spanish Territories

Claimed by Great Britain, Spain, and the U.S.

BRITISH NORTH AMERICA

Vt.

NH

Mass.

Rhode Island

Conn.

New Jersey

Delaware

Maryland

New York

Pennsylvania

Virginia

North Carolina

South Carolina

Georgia

Atlantic Ocean

MICHIGAN TERR.

Ohio

Kentucky

Tennessee

INDIANA TERRITORY

MISSISSIPPI TERRITORY

SPANISH FLORIDA

Gulf of Mexico

LOUISIANA PURCHASE 1803

ROCKY MOUNTAINS

OREGON COUNTRY

(Claimed by Great Britain, Spain, and the U.S.)

SPANISH TERRITORY

Pacific Ocean

Name: _____

Date: _____

Lewis and Clark Expedition, 1804–1806

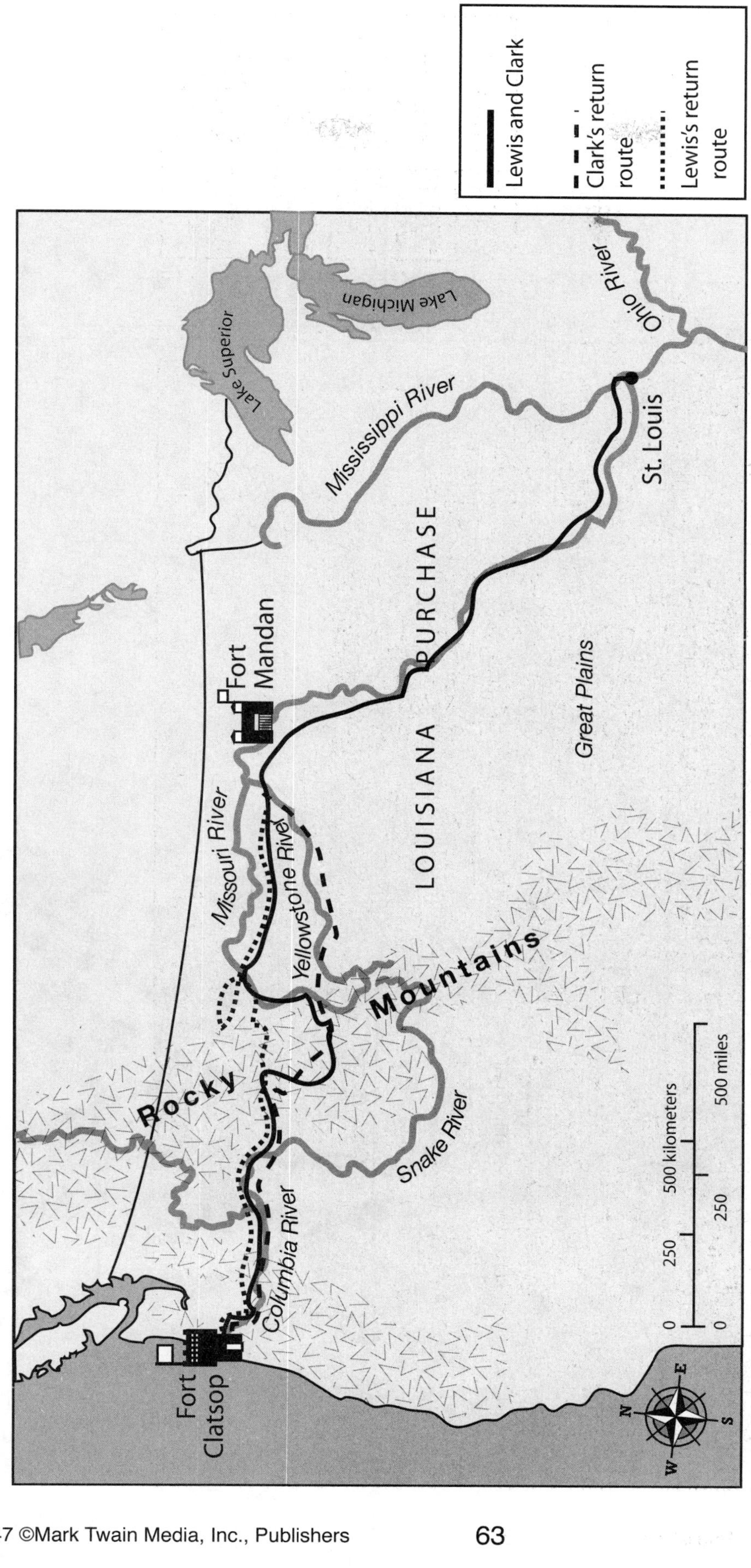

Map #: 053

Legend:
- Lewis and Clark
- Clark's return route
- Lewis's return route

Lake Superior

Lake Michigan

Mississippi River

Ohio River

St. Louis

Fort Mandan

LOUISIANA PURCHASE

Great Plains

Missouri River

Yellowstone River

Rocky Mountains

Snake River

Columbia River

Fort Clatsop

500 kilometers   250   0
500 miles   250   0

N E S W

Name: _____

Date: _____

War of 1812 With Troop Movements and Battles

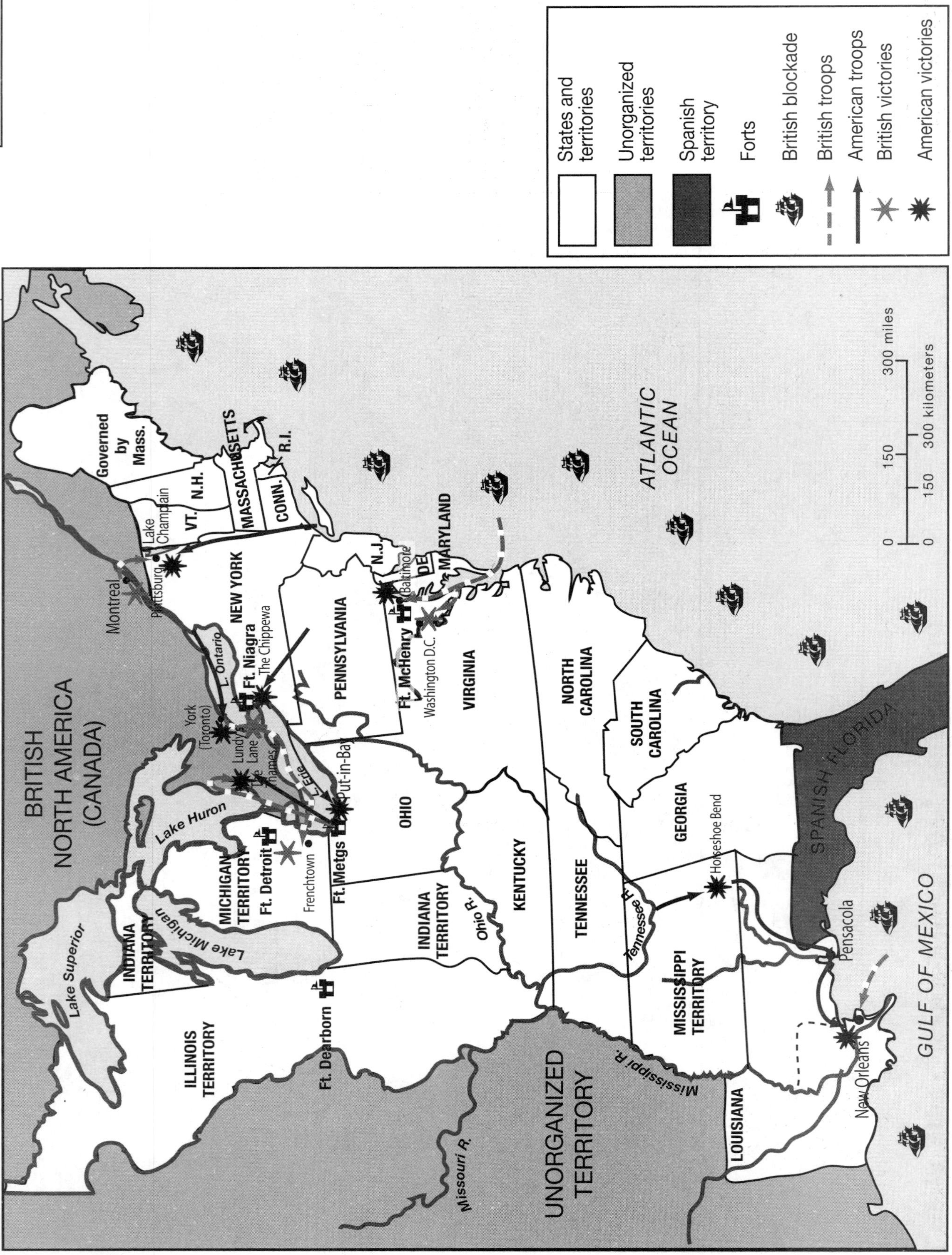

Map #: 054

Legend:
- States and territories
- Unorganized territories
- Spanish territory
- Forts
- British blockade
- British troops
- American troops
- British victories
- American victories

- 300 miles
- 300 kilometers
- 150
- 0

Map labels:

BRITISH NORTH AMERICA (CANADA)

Lake Superior

Lake Huron

Lake Michigan

L. Ontario

L. Erie

Montreal

Plattsburg

Lake Champlain

York (Toronto)

Lundy's Lane

The Thames

Put-in-Bay

Ft. Niagra

The Chippewa

Governed by Mass.

VT.

N.H.

MASSACHUSETTS

CONN.

R.I.

NEW YORK

PENNSYLVANIA

N.J.

DE

MARYLAND

Baltimore

Ft. McHenry

Washington D.C.

VIRGINIA

NORTH CAROLINA

SOUTH CAROLINA

GEORGIA

Horseshoe Bend

ATLANTIC OCEAN

Frenchtown

Ft. Detroit

MICHIGAN TERRITORY

Ft. Metgs

OHIO

INDIANA TERRITORY

Ohio R.

KENTUCKY

TENNESSEE

Tennessee R.

MISSISSIPPI TERRITORY

Pensacola

SPANISH FLORIDA

GULF OF MEXICO

New Orleans

LOUISIANA

Mississippi R.

UNORGANIZED TERRITORY

Ft. Dearborn

ILLINOIS TERRITORY

INDIANA TERRITORY

Missouri R.

Name: _____

Date: _____

Westward Expansion, 1815–1845

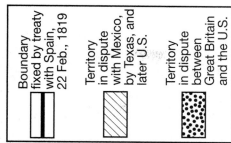

	Boundary fixed by treaty with Spain, 22 Feb., 1819
	Territory in dispute with Mexico, by Texas, and later U.S.
	Territory in dispute between Great Britain and the U.S.

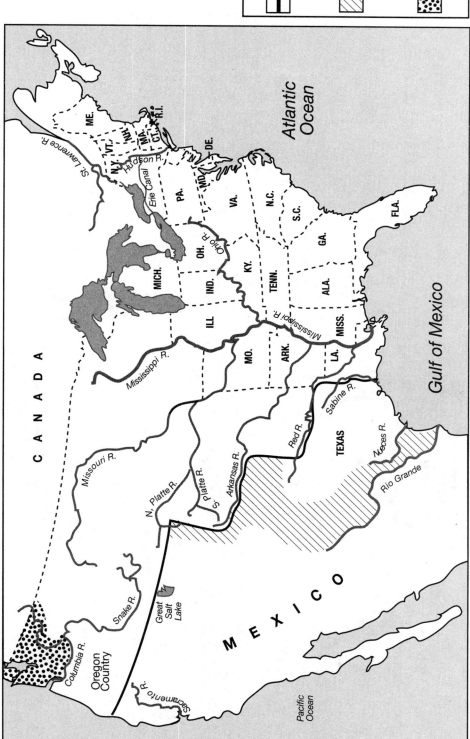

CANADA

St. Lawrence R.

ME.

VT. NH. MA. CT. R.I.

N.Y.

Hudson R.

Erie Canal

PA.

MD.

N.J.

DE.

Atlantic Ocean

OH.

Ohio R.

VA.

N.C.

MICH.

IND.

KY.

S.C.

ILL.

TENN.

GA.

Mississippi R.

ALA.

FLA.

Missouri R.

MO.

ARK.

MISS.

LA.

Mississippi R.

N. Platte R.

S. Platte R.

Arkansas R.

Red R.

Sabine R.

Nueces R.

TEXAS

Rio Grande

Gulf of Mexico

Snake R.

Great Salt Lake

MEXICO

Columbia R.

Oregon Country

Sacramento R.

Pacific Ocean

Name: _____

Date: _____

Acquisition of Florida, 1819

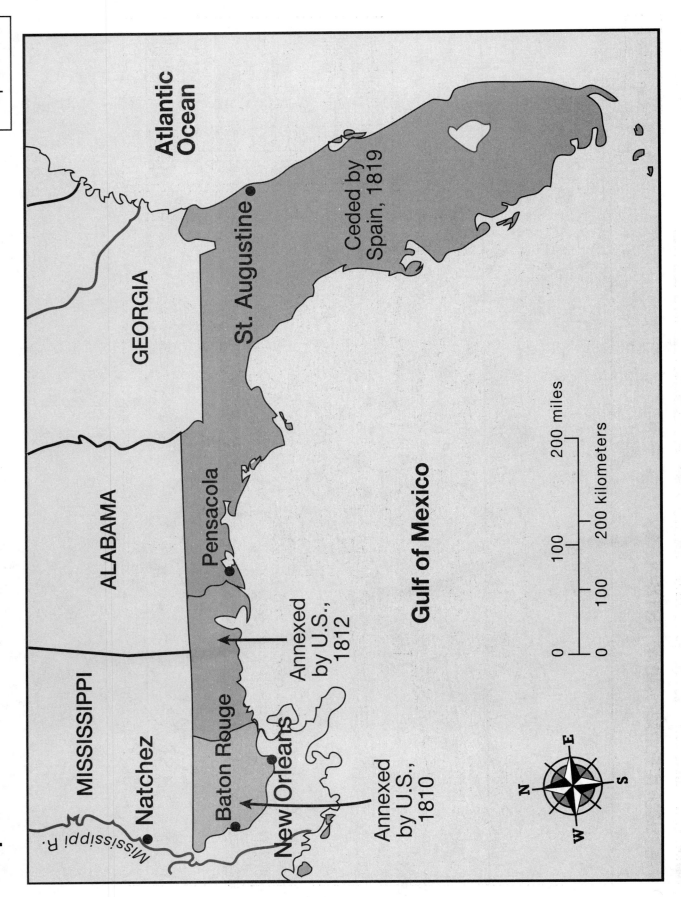

Atlantic Ocean

GEORGIA

St. Augustine

Ceded by Spain, 1819

ALABAMA

Pensacola

MISSISSIPPI

Natchez

Baton Rouge

New Orleans

Mississippi R.

Annexed by U.S., 1812

Annexed by U.S., 1810

Gulf of Mexico

200 miles

200 kilometers

0   100   100   200

N E S W

Name: _____

Date: _____

Missouri Compromise, 1820

Map #: 057

Legend:

- Slave States
- Free states & territories
- Open to slavery by the Missouri Compromise
- Closed to slavery by the Missouri Compromise
- Claimed by Great Britain, Spain, and the U.S.

BRITISH NORTH AMERICA (CANADA)

OREGON COUNTRY
Joint U.S.-British occupation of disputed territory

UNORGANIZED TERRITORY

36° 30' Missouri Compromise line

MISSOURI Admitted as slave state 1821

ARKANSAS TERRITORY

NEW SPAIN (Independent Mexico, 1821)

MICHIGAN TERRITORY

Great Lakes

OHIO

IN

IL

KY.

TENNESSEE

MISS.

ALA.

LA.

MAINE Admitted as free state 1820

VT.

N.H.

MA.

R.I.

CONN.

N.Y.

PA.

N.J.

DEL.

MD.

D.C.

VA.

N.C.

S.C.

GA.

FLORIDA TERRITORY

Atlantic Ocean

Gulf of Mexico

Pacific Ocean

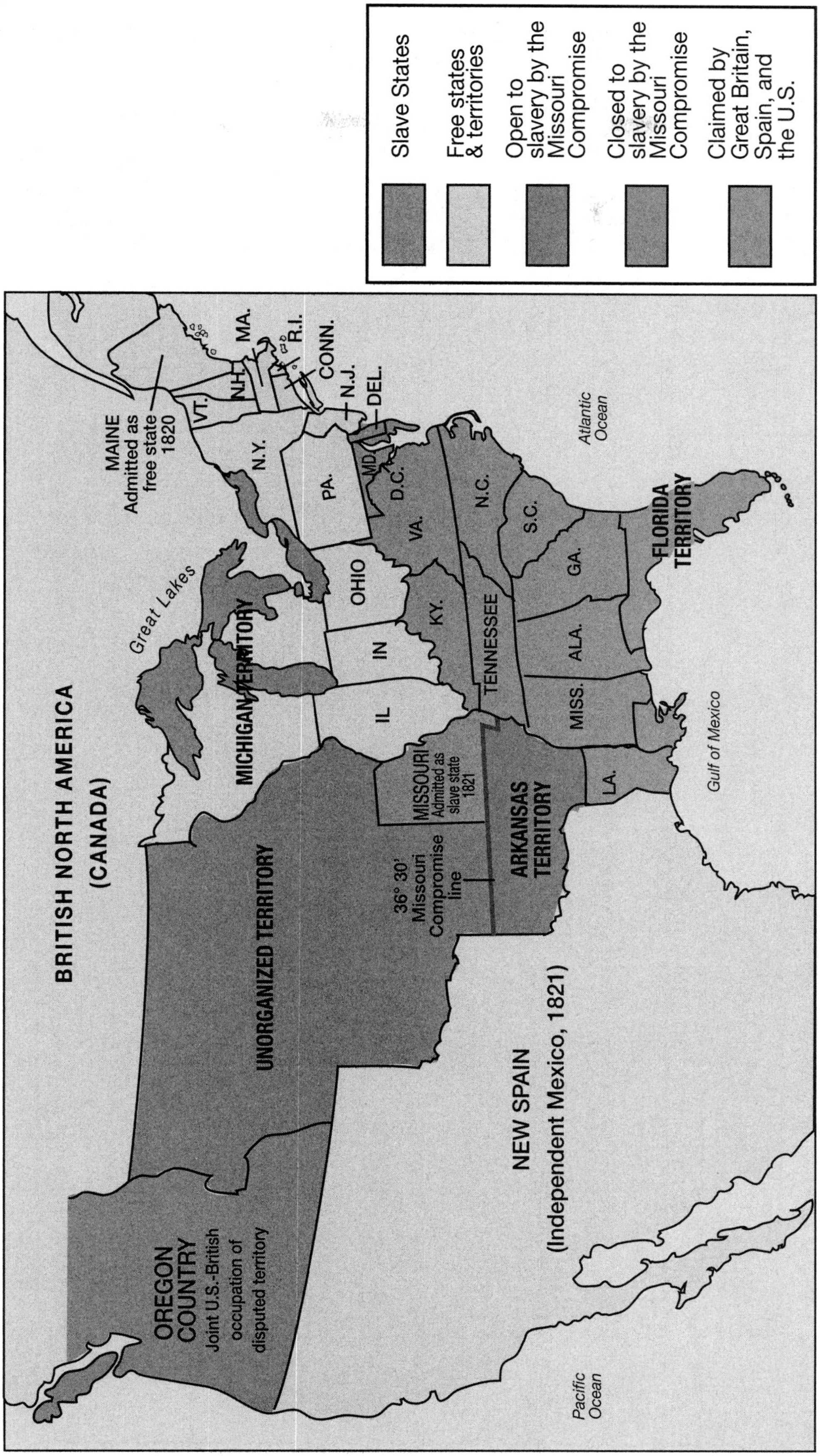

Name: _____

Date: _____

Removal of Native Americans, 1820–1840

Map #: 058

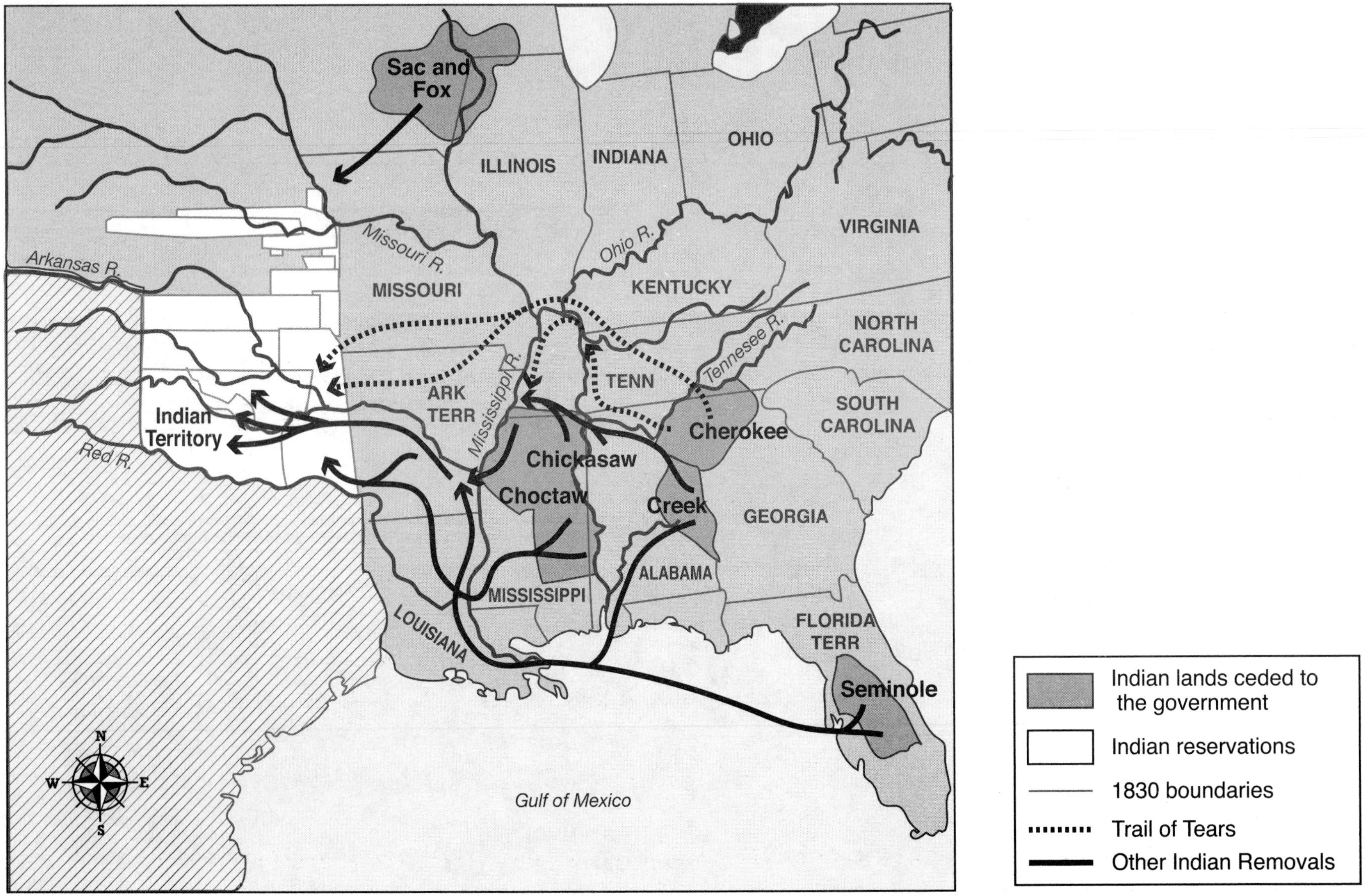

Legend:
- Indian lands ceded to the government
- Indian reservations
- 1830 boundaries
- Trail of Tears
- Other Indian Removals

VIRGINIA

NORTH CAROLINA

SOUTH CAROLINA

OHIO

KENTUCKY

TENN

Cherokee

GEORGIA

ALABAMA

FLORIDA TERR

Seminole

Tennessee R.

Ohio R.

INDIANA

ILLINOIS

Chickasaw

Choctaw

Creek

MISSISSIPPI

LOUISIANA

Gulf of Mexico

Mississippi R.

Sac and Fox

MISSOURI

Missouri R.

ARK TERR

Indian Territory

Arkansas R.

Red R.

Name: _____

Date: _____

Trail of Tears and the Cherokee Removal, 1830s

Map #: 059

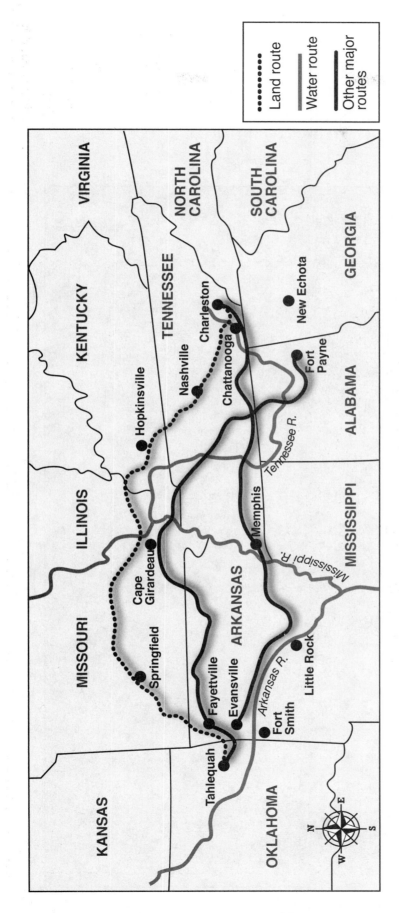

Legend:
- ••••• Land route
- ——— Water route
- ━━━ Other major routes

Name: _____

Date: _____

Western Trails

Map #: 060

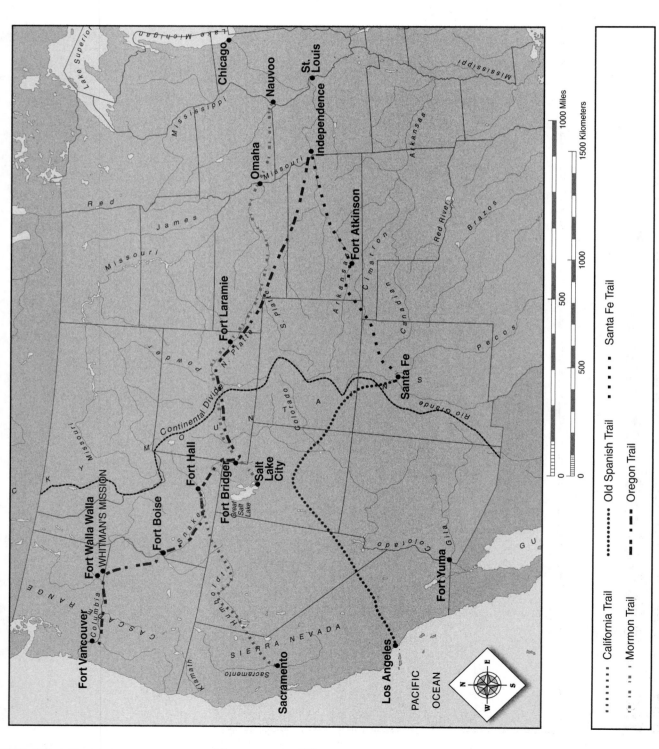

California Trail ....

Old Spanish Trail ••••••••••

Santa Fe Trail ••••••••

Mormon Trail •• ·• ·• ··

Oregon Trail ·• ·• ·•

Name: _____

Date: _____

The Santa Fe Trail

Map #: 061

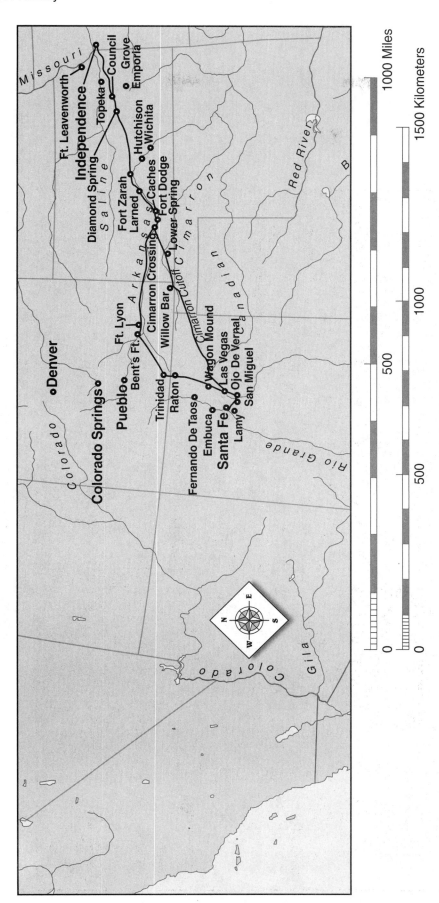

Name: _____

Date: _____

The Oregon Trail

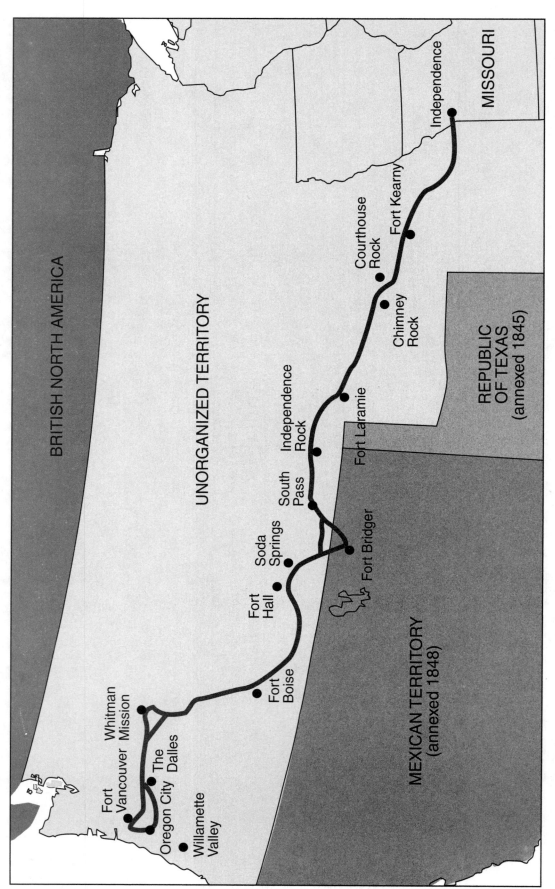

Route of the Oregon Trail

Name: _____

Date: _____

The Oregon Trail With State Borders

Map #: 062.1

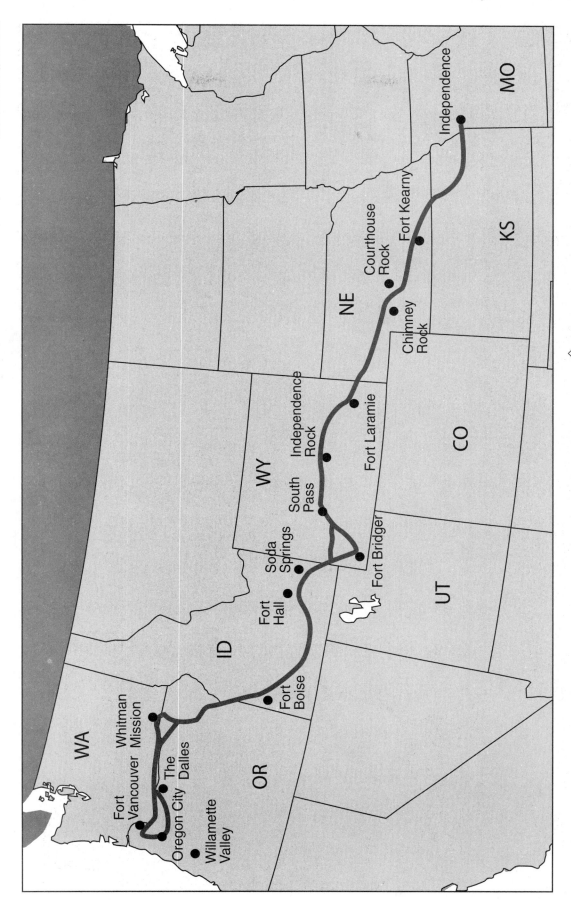

Route of the Oregon Trail

Name: _____

Date: _____

The Mormon Trail

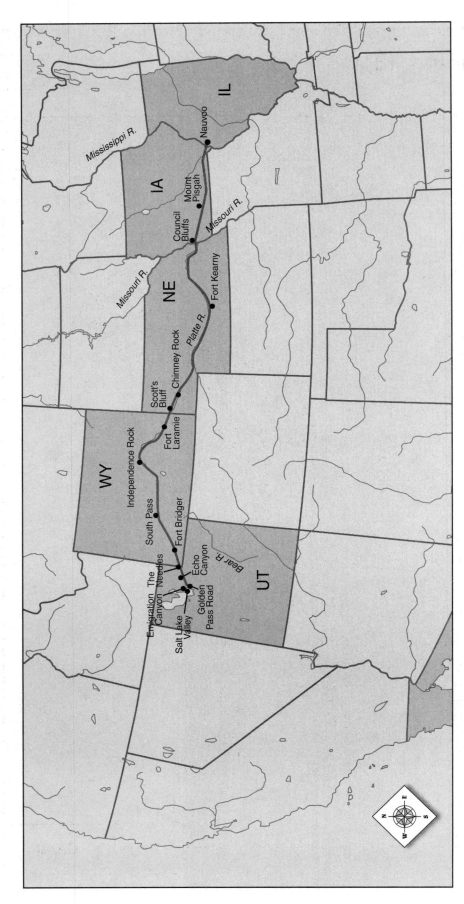

IL

Nauvoo

Mississippi R.

IA

Mount Pisgah

Council Bluffs

Missouri R.

Missouri R.

NE

Fort Kearny

Platte R.

Chimney Rock

Scott's Bluff

Fort Laramie

Independence Rock

WY

South Pass

Fort Bridger

Echo Canyon

Emigration The Canyon Needles

Bear R.

Golden Pass Road

Salt Lake Valley

UT

Name: _____ Date: _____

Important Canals, 1840

Map #: 064

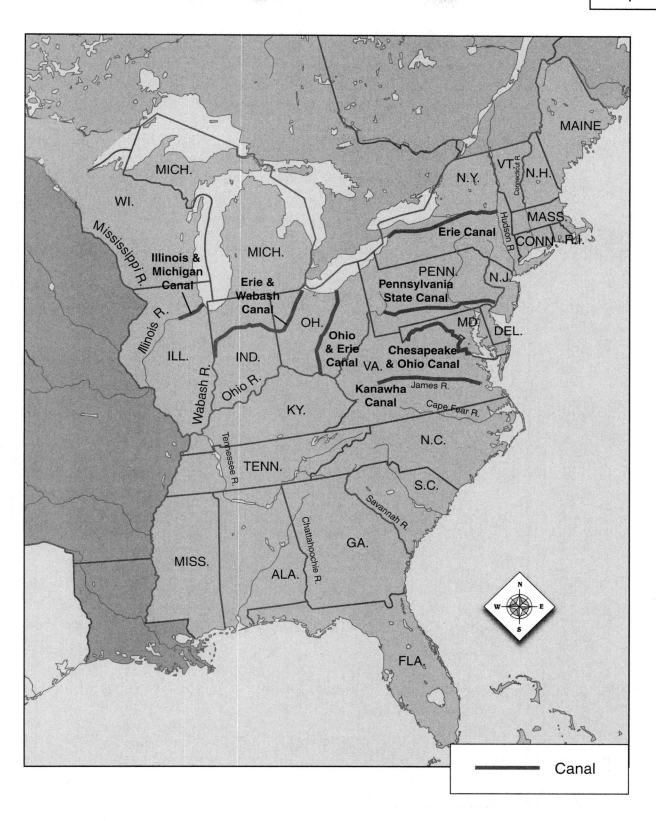

Name: _____

Date: _____

Texas War for Independence With Troop Movements and Battles

Map #: 065

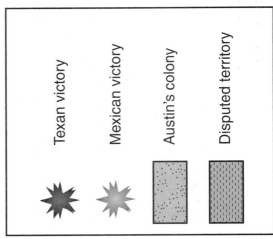

Texan victory

Mexican victory

Austin's colony

Disputed territory

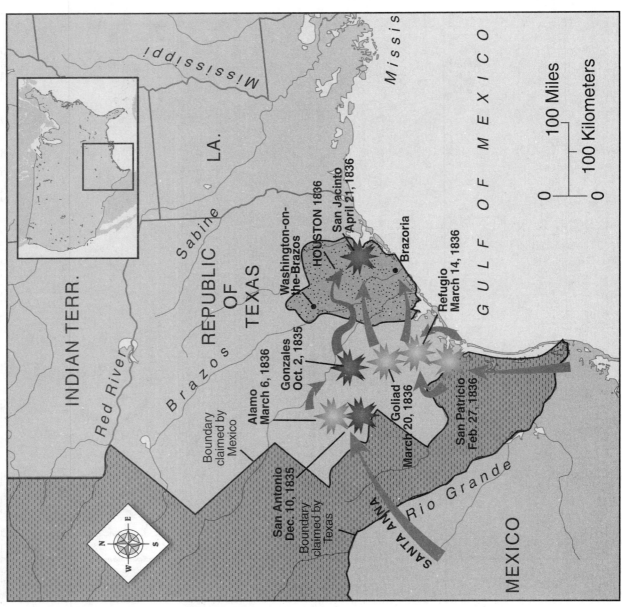

INDIAN TERR.

Red River

Mississippi

LA.

Sabine

REPUBLIC OF TEXAS

Brazos

Boundary claimed by Mexico

Washington-on-the-Brazos

HOUSTON 1836

San Jacinto April 21, 1836

Brazoria

Missis

Refugio March 14, 1836

GULF OF MEXICO

Gonzales Oct. 2, 1835

Alamo March 6, 1836

San Antonio Dec. 10, 1835

Boundary claimed by Texas

Goliad March 20, 1836

San Patricio Feb. 27, 1836

SANTA ANNA

Rio Grande

MEXICO

100 Miles

100 Kilometers

Oregon Country

Name: _____

Date: _____

Map #: 066

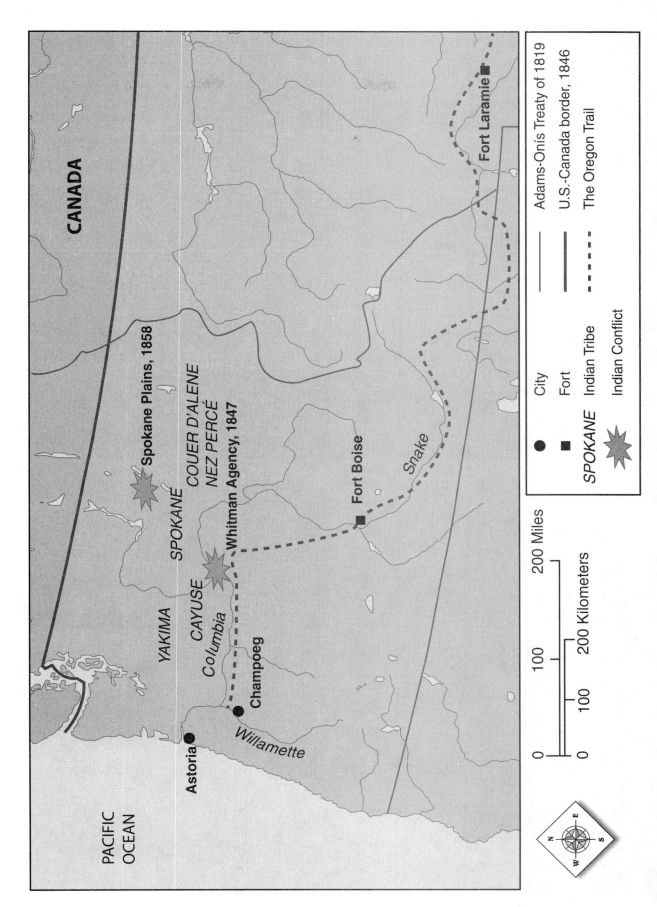

PACIFIC
OCEAN

CANADA

Astoria

Willamette

Champoeg

Columbia

CAYUSE

YAKIMA

SPOKANE

COUER D'ALENE

NEZ PERCÉ

Whitman Agency, 1847

Spokane Plains, 1858

Fort Boise

Snake

Fort Laramie

Legend:

- ● City
- ■ Fort
- *SPOKANE* Indian Tribe
- ✴ Indian Conflict

- ——— Adams-Onís Treaty of 1819
- ——— U.S.-Canada border, 1846
- - - - The Oregon Trail

0   100   200 Miles

0   100   200 Kilometers

N E S W

Name: _____ Date: _____

Northwest Boundary Established

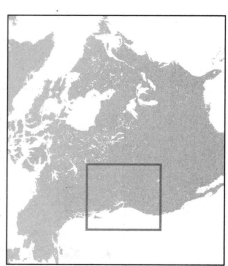

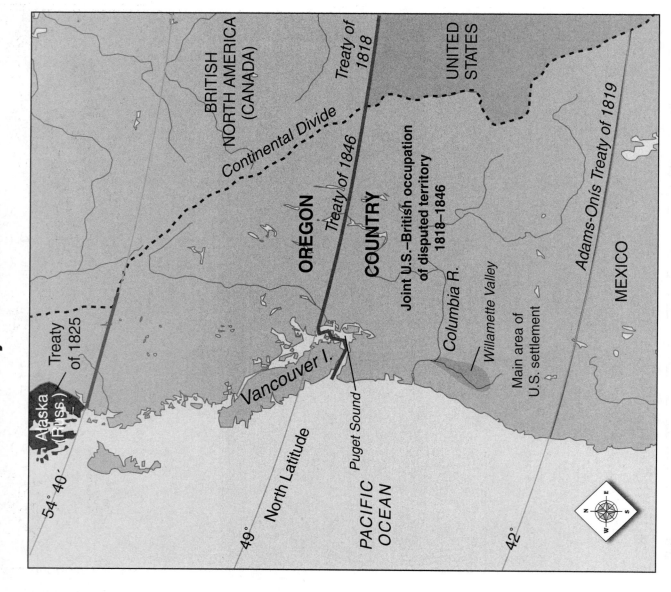

BRITISH
NORTH AMERICA
(CANADA)

Treaty of 1818

Continental Divide

UNITED
STATES

OREGON

Treaty of 1846

COUNTRY

Joint U.S.–British occupation
of disputed territory
1818–1846

Columbia R.

Willamette Valley

Adams-Onís Treaty of 1819

Main area of
U.S. settlement

MEXICO

Treaty of 1825

Alaska
(RUالسيا.)

54° 40'

Vancouver I.

Puget Sound

North Latitude

49°

PACIFIC
OCEAN

42°

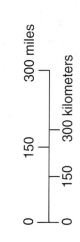

300 miles

150

0

300 kilometers

150

0

Name: _____

Date: _____

The War With Mexico, 1846–1848:
Famous Battles With Troop Movements

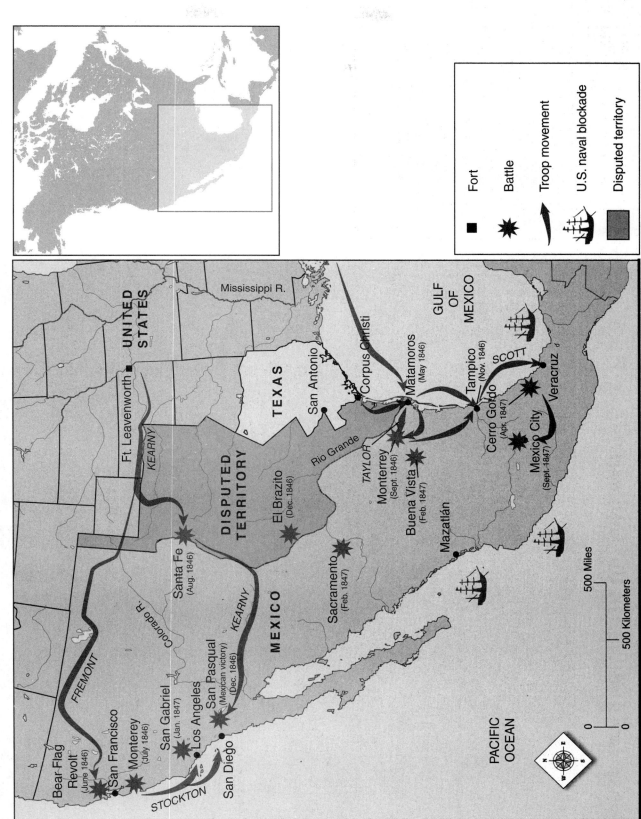

UNITED STATES

Mississippi R.

Ft. Leavenworth

KEARNY

TEXAS

San Antonio

Corpus Christi

Rio Grande

TAYLOR

DISPUTED TERRITORY

El Brazito
(Dec. 1846)

Matamoros
(May 1846)

Monterrey
(Sept. 1846)

Buena Vista
(Feb. 1847)

Tampico
(Nov. 1846)

SCOTT

Cerro Gordo
(Apr. 1847)

Veracruz

Mexico City
(Sept. 1847)

GULF OF MEXICO

Santa Fe
(Aug. 1846)

KEARNY

MEXICO

Sacramento
(Feb. 1847)

Mazatlán

San Gabriel
(Jan. 1847)

Los Angeles

San Pasqual
(Mexican victory)
(Dec. 1846)

FREMONT

Colorado R.

Bear-Flag
Revolt
(June 1846)

San Francisco

Monterey
(July 1846)

San Diego

STOCKTON

PACIFIC OCEAN

0   500 Miles

0   500 Kilometers

N E S W

Legend

Fort ■	
Battle ✸	
Troop movement	
U.S. naval blockade	
Disputed territory	

Name:

Date:

Major Gold Strikes in the California Gold Rush, 1848–1859

Map #: 069

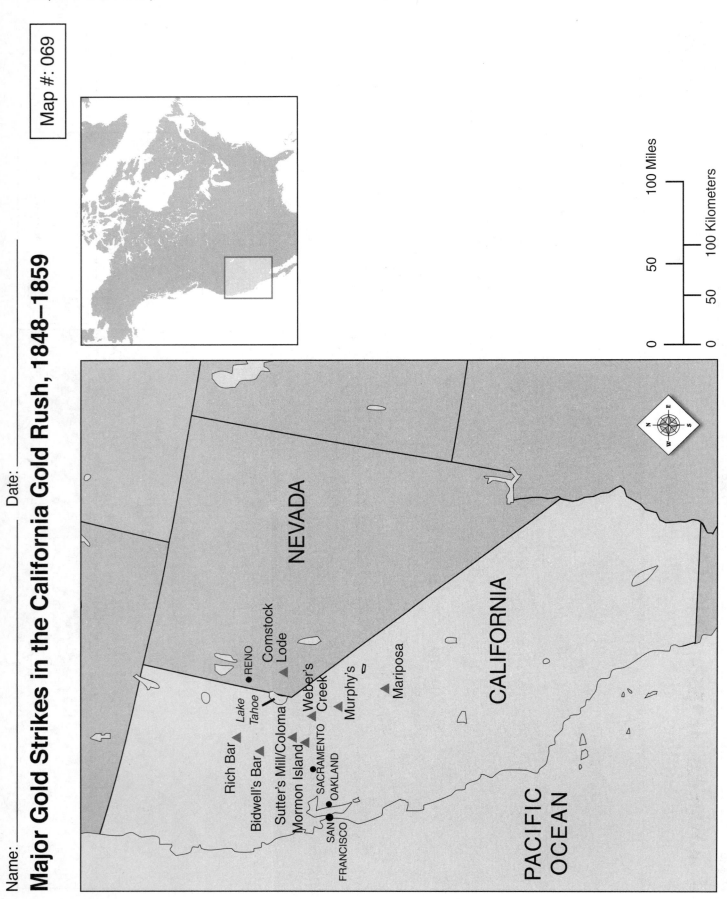

NEVADA

CALIFORNIA

PACIFIC OCEAN

RENO

Lake Tahoe

Comstock Lode

Weber's Creek

Murphy's

Mariposa

Rich Bar

Bidwell's Bar

Sutter's Mill/Coloma

Mormon Island

SACRAMENTO

OAKLAND

SAN FRANCISCO

100 Miles

50

0

100 Kilometers

50

0

Name: _____

Date: _____

Compromise of 1850

Free states & territories

Slave states

Slavery determined by popular sovereignty

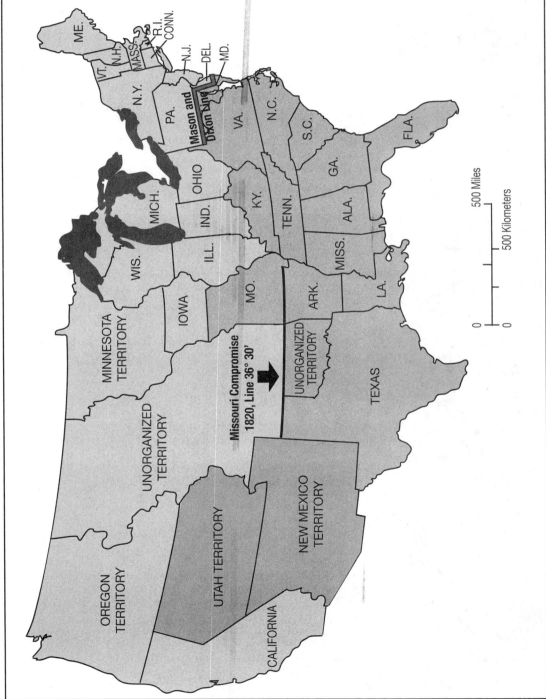

Name: _____

Date: _____

Kansas-Nebraska Act, 1854

Map #: 071

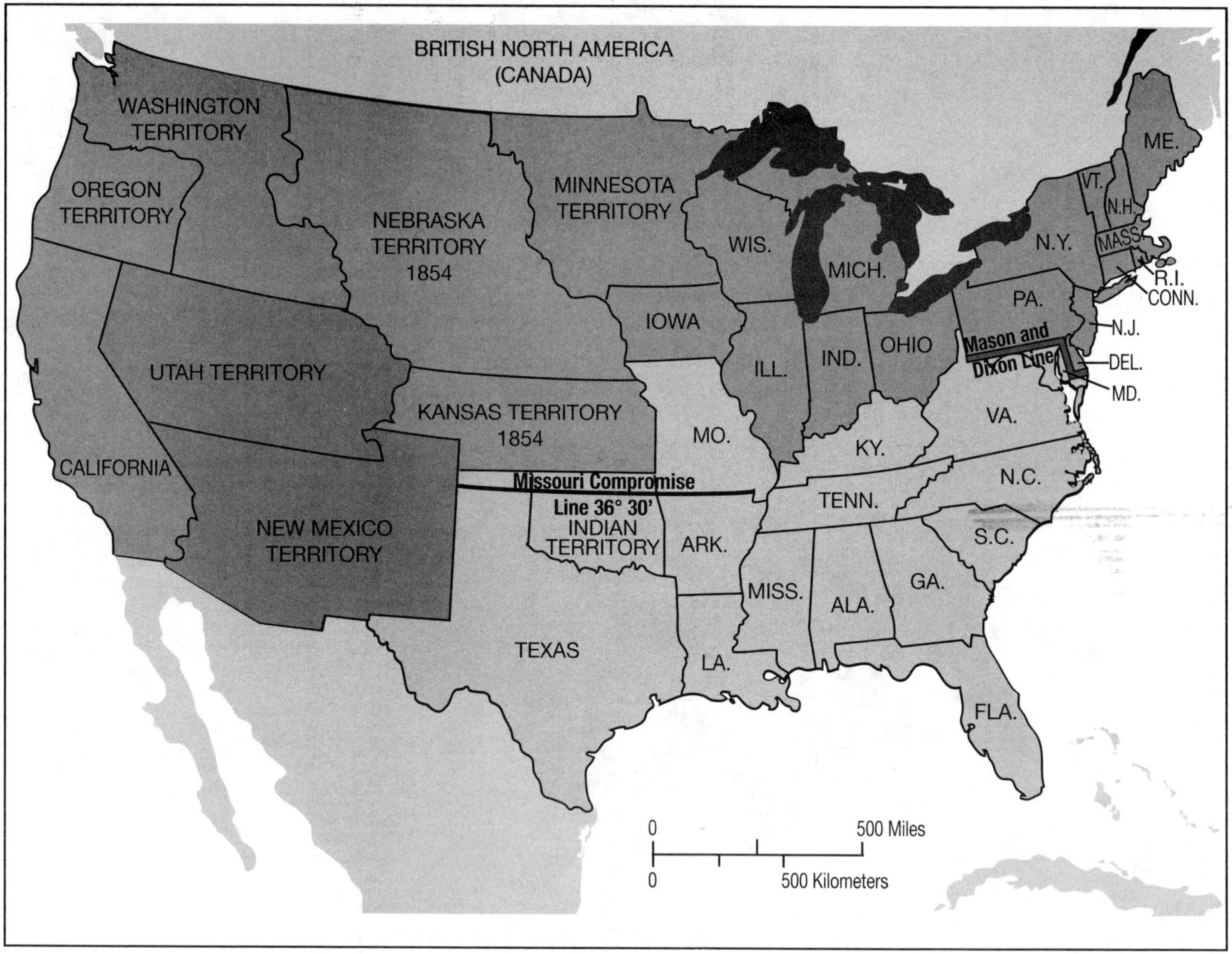

Free state or territory

Slave state or territory

Opened to slavery by principle of popular sovereignty, compromise of 1850

Opened to slavery by principle of popular sovereignty, Kansas-Nebraska Act of 1854

BRITISH NORTH AMERICA (CANADA)

WASHINGTON TERRITORY

OREGON TERRITORY

MINNESOTA TERRITORY

NEBRASKA TERRITORY 1854

UTAH TERRITORY

KANSAS TERRITORY 1854

CALIFORNIA

NEW MEXICO TERRITORY

TEXAS

INDIAN TERRITORY

Missouri Compromise Line 36° 30'

IOWA

WIS.

ILL.

MO.

ARK.

LA.

MICH.

IND.

OHIO

KY.

TENN.

MISS.

ALA.

GA.

S.C.

N.C.

VA.

FLA.

ME.

VT.

N.H.

MASS.

R.I.

CONN.

N.Y.

PA.

N.J.

DEL.

MD.

Mason and Dixon Line

500 Miles

500 Kilometers

Name: _____   Date: _____

Bleeding Kansas, 1854–1858

Map #: 072

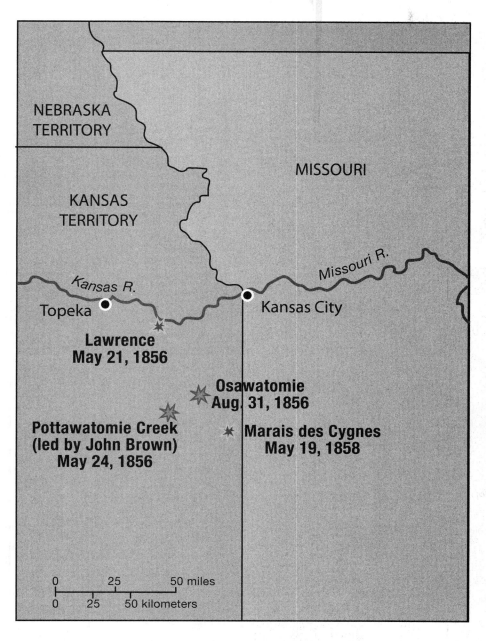

NEBRASKA
TERRITORY

MISSOURI

KANSAS
TERRITORY

Missouri R.

Kansas R.

Topeka

Kansas City

**Lawrence
May 21, 1856**

**Osawatomie
Aug. 31, 1856**

**Pottawatomie Creek
(led by John Brown)
May 24, 1856**

**Marais des Cygnes
May 19, 1858**

```
0        25        50 miles
0     25      50 kilometers
```

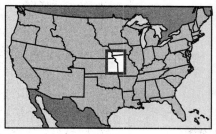

 Attacks by
free-state forces

 Attacks by
pro-slavery forces

Map #: 073

Name: _____

Date: _____

Voting Rights of Men Prior to 1855

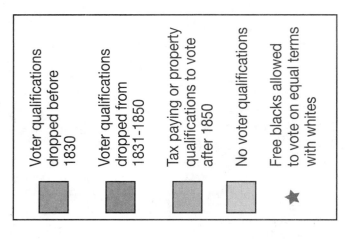

Voter qualifications dropped before 1830

Voter qualifications dropped from 1831–1850

Tax paying or property qualifications to vote after 1850

No voter qualifications

★ Free blacks allowed to vote on equal terms with whites

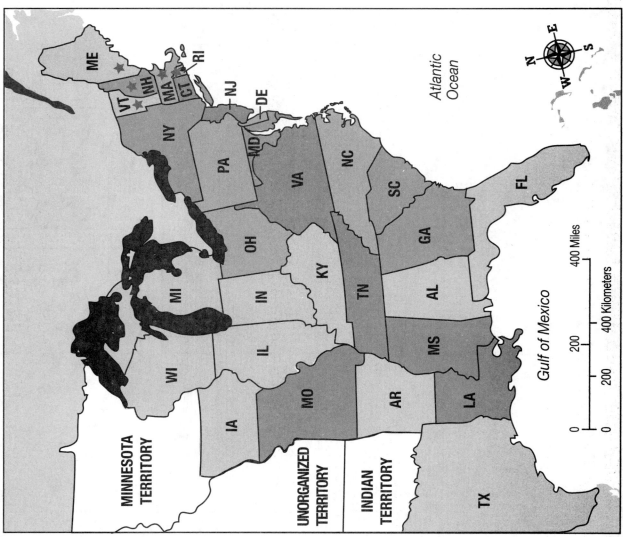

Name: _____

Date: _____

United States in 1856: Free States, Slave States, and Territories

Map #: 074

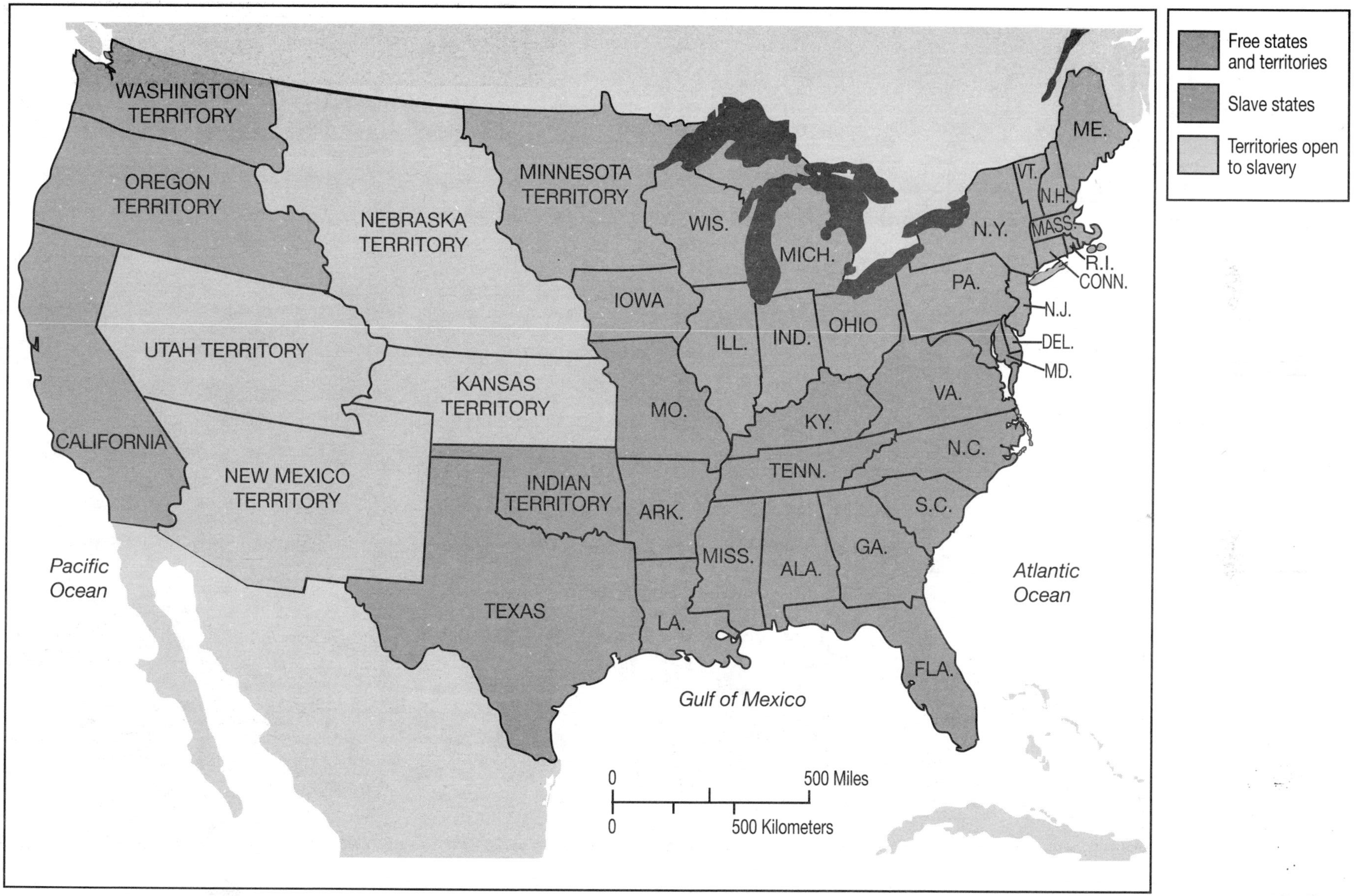

Legend:
- Free states and territories
- Slave states
- Territories open to slavery

Atlantic Ocean

Pacific Ocean

Gulf of Mexico

ME.
VT.
N.H.
MASS.
R.I.
CONN.
N.Y.
N.J.
PA.
DEL.
MD.
VA.
N.C.
S.C.
FLA.
GA.
ALA.
MISS.
LA.
OHIO
IND.
ILL.
KY.
TENN.
ARK.
MICH.
WIS.
IOWA
MO.
TEXAS
INDIAN TERRITORY
MINNESOTA TERRITORY
KANSAS TERRITORY
NEBRASKA TERRITORY
NEW MEXICO TERRITORY
UTAH TERRITORY
CALIFORNIA
OREGON TERRITORY
WASHINGTON TERRITORY

500 Miles

500 Kilometers

Name: _____

Date: _____

States and Territories of the United States, 1858–1859

Map #: 075

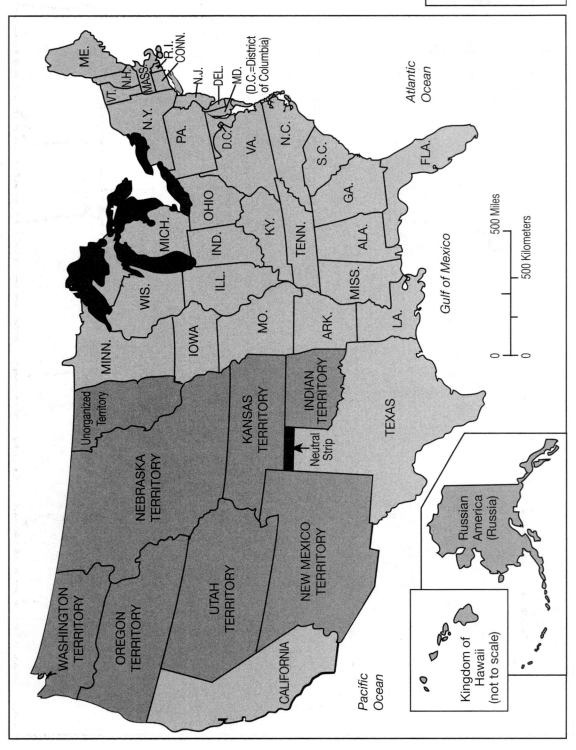

States
Territories
Other countries
Disputed areas

ME.

N.H.

VT.

MASS.

R.I.

CONN.

N.Y.

N.J.

PA.

DEL.

MD.

(D.C.=District of Columbia)

D.C.

VA.

N.C.

S.C.

FLA.

GA.

ALA.

MISS.

OHIO

IND.

ILL.

KY.

TENN.

MICH.

WIS.

IOWA

MINN.

MO.

ARK.

LA.

TEXAS

Unorganized Territory

NEBRASKA TERRITORY

KANSAS TERRITORY

INDIAN TERRITORY

Neutral Strip

WASHINGTON TERRITORY

OREGON TERRITORY

UTAH TERRITORY

NEW MEXICO TERRITORY

CALIFORNIA

Atlantic Ocean

Gulf of Mexico

Pacific Ocean

500 Miles

500 Kilometers

Russian America (Russia)

Kingdom of Hawaii (not to scale)

Name: _____

Date: _____

Pony Express Route

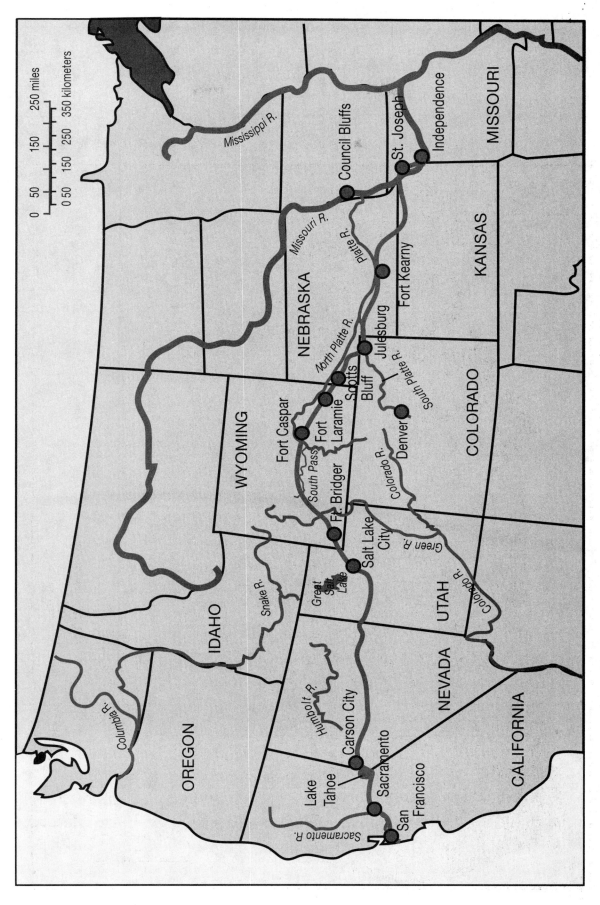

Name: _____ Date: _____

The Underground Railroad

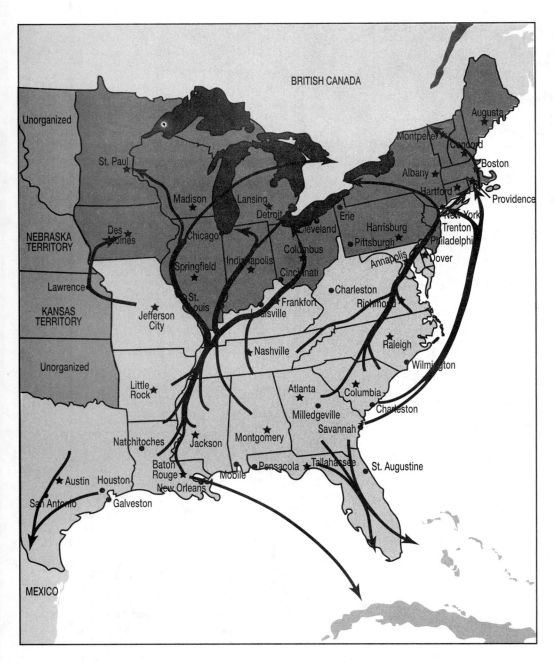

Legend:

- Free states
- Slave holding states
- Territories
- Major routes of escape

BRITISH CANADA

Augusta
Montpelier
Concord
Boston
St. Paul
Albany
Hartford
Providence
Madison
Lansing
Detroit
Erie
New York
Cleveland
Trenton
Harrisburg
Chicago
Columbus
Pittsburgh
Philadelphia
Des Moines
NEBRASKA TERRITORY
Springfield
Indianapolis
Cincinnati
Annapolis
Dover
Lawrence
St. Louis
Frankfort
Louisville
Charleston
Richmond
KANSAS TERRITORY
Jefferson City
Nashville
Raleigh
Wilmington
Unorganized
Little Rock
Atlanta
Columbia
Charleston
Milledgeville
Natchitoches
Jackson
Montgomery
Savannah
Baton Rouge
Mobile
Pensacola
Tallahassee
St. Augustine
Austin
Houston
San Antonio
Galveston
New Orleans
MEXICO

Name: _____

Date: _____

Cotton Production in the South, 1820

Map #: 078

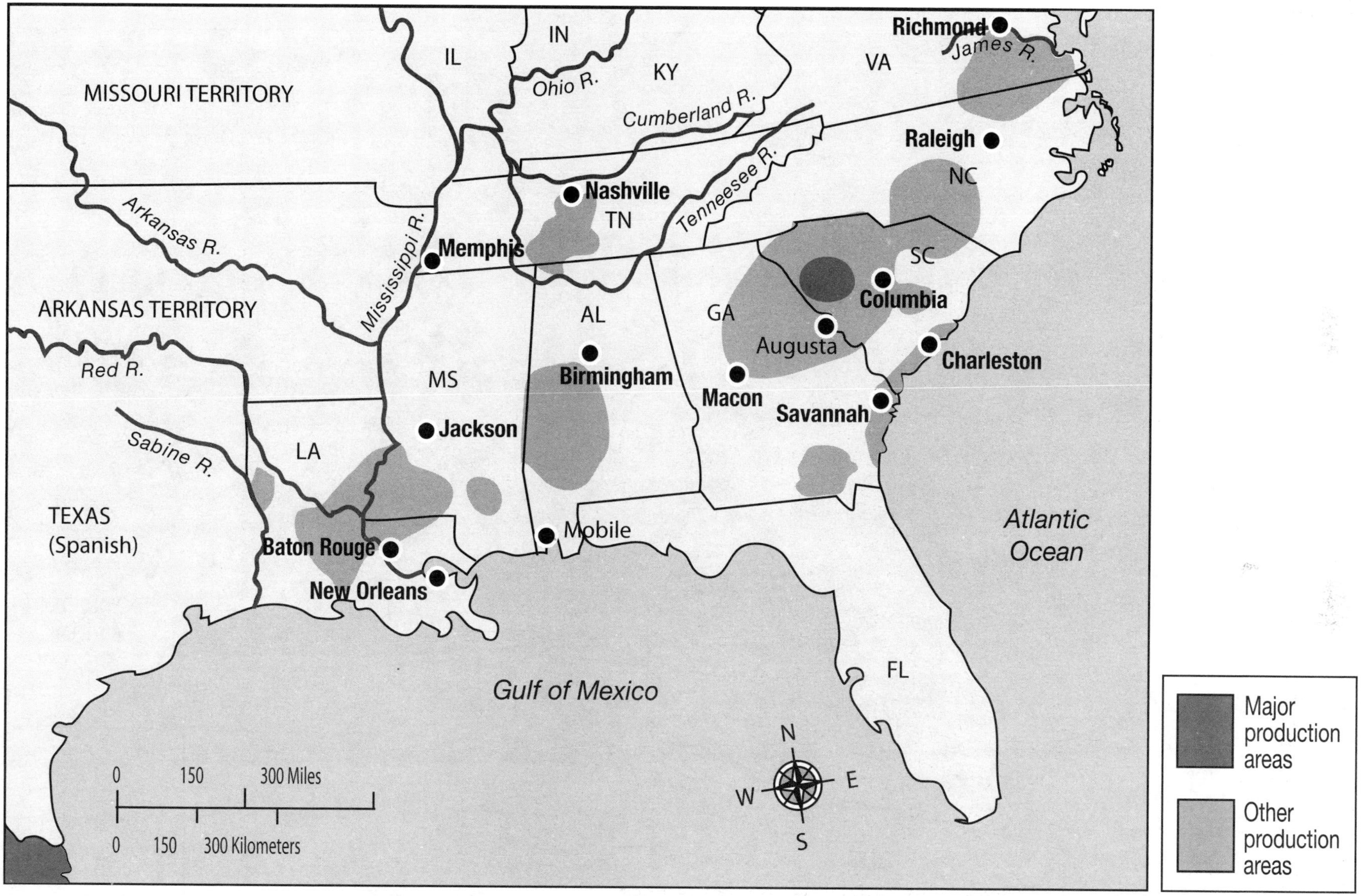

Legend:
- Major production areas
- Other production areas

Atlantic Ocean

Richmond
James R.
Raleigh
NC
VA
SC
Charleston
Columbia
Augusta
Savannah
GA
Macon

FL

KY
Cumberland R.
Tennessee R.
IN
Ohio R.
Nashville
TN
AL
Birmingham
Mobile

Gulf of Mexico

IL
Memphis
Mississippi R.
MS
Jackson
New Orleans
Baton Rouge
LA

MISSOURI TERRITORY
Arkansas R.
ARKANSAS TERRITORY
Red R.
Sabine R.
TEXAS (Spanish)

Compass: N E S W

Scale:
300 Miles
300 Kilometers
0 150 300

Name: _____

Date: _____

Cotton Production in the South, 1860

Map #: 079

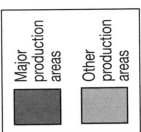

Major production areas

Other production areas

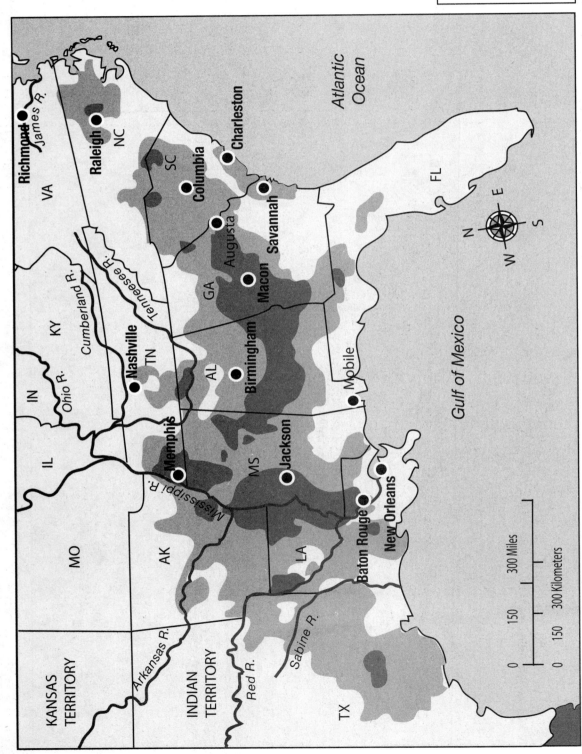

Name: _____

Date: _____

Resources of the Northern and Southern States Before 1860

Map #: 080

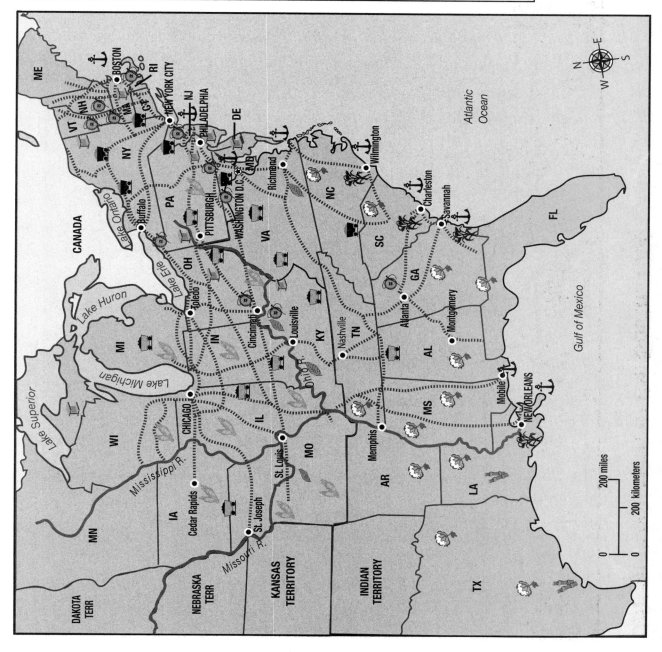

Legend:

- Northern states & territories
- Southern states & territories
- Port
- Railroad
- Coal
- Cotton
- Iron & steel works
- Iron ore
- Rice
- Sugar cane
- Textile manufacturing
- Tobacco
- Wheat

200 miles

200 kilometers

Name: _____

Date: _____

U.S. Cities, 1860

Population of Cities
- ■ More than 250,000
- ● 50,000 – 250,000
- Mason-Dixon Line

British Possessions

ME
VT
NH
MA
CT
RI
NY
Albany
Boston
Providence
Brooklyn
New York
Newark
NJ
DE
Baltimore
MD
Philadelphia
PA
Washington, D.C.
VA
NC
SC
GA
FL
Buffalo
OH
Cincinnati
KY
Louisville
TN
AL
MI
IN
Chicago
IL
MS
New Orleans
LA
AR
St. Louis
MO
IA
MN
WI
TERRITORIES
TX
Mexico
CA
San Francisco
OR

Atlantic Ocean

Gulf of Mexico

Pacific Ocean

500 Miles

500 Kilometers

Name: _____

Date: _____

Slave Population Density, 1860

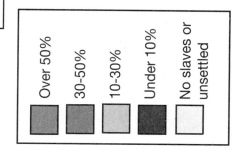

Over 50%

30-50%

10-30%

Under 10%

No slaves or unsettled

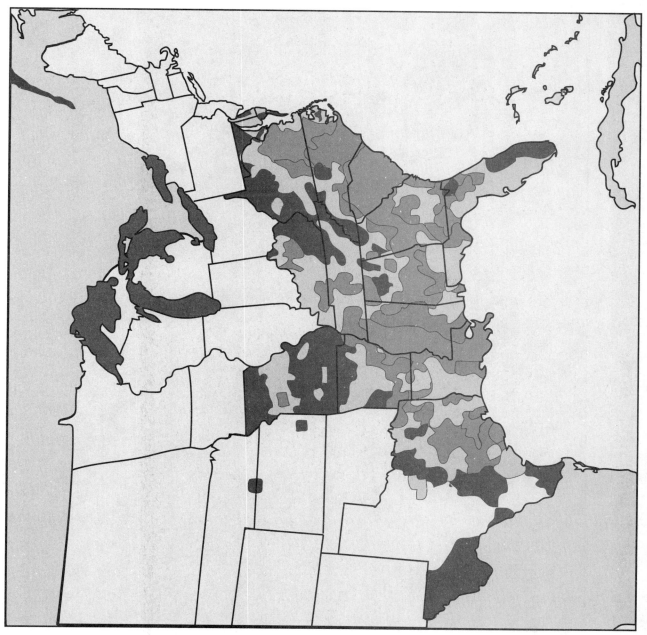

Name: _____

Date: _____

Population Density, 1860

Map #: 083

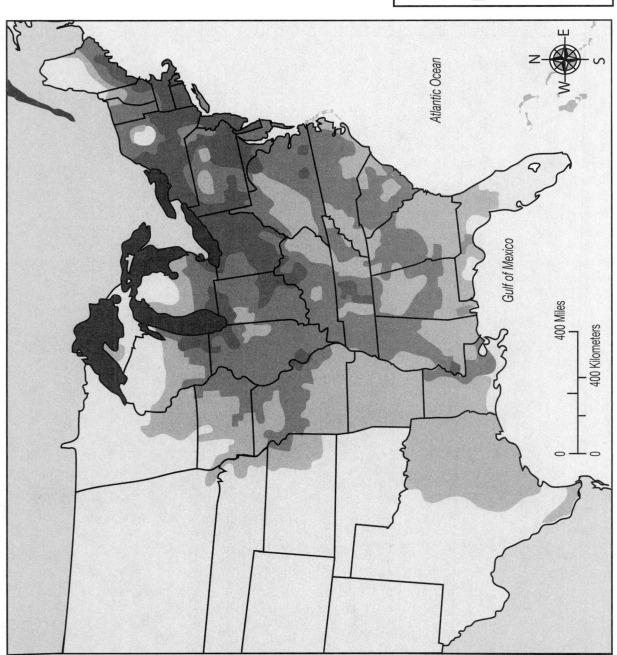

People per square mile | People per square kilometer

People per square mile	People per square kilometer
More than 45	More than 18
18–45	8–18
2–18	1–8
Less than 2	Less than 1

Atlantic Ocean

Gulf of Mexico

400 Miles

400 Kilometers

Name: _____

Date: _____

Election of 1860

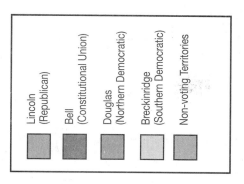

Map #: 084

Lincoln
(Republican)

Bell
(Constitutional Union)

Douglas
(Northern Democratic)

Breckinridge
(Southern Democratic)

Non-voting Territories

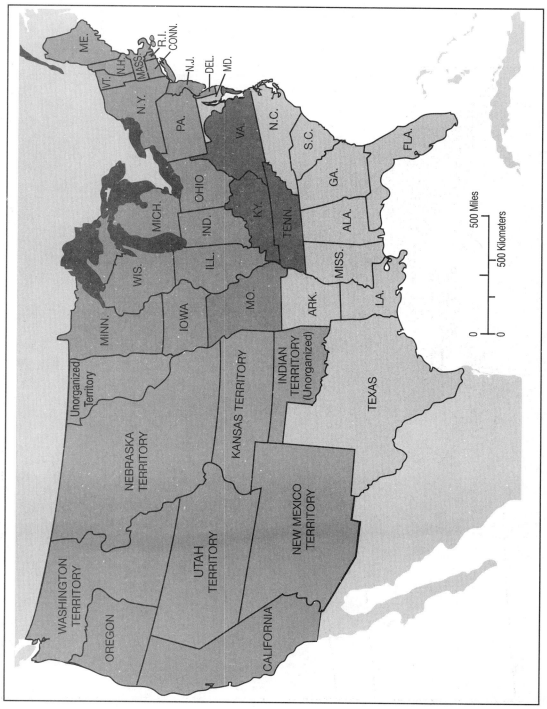

500 Miles

500 Kilometers

Name: _____

Date: _____

Railroads Prior to the Civil War

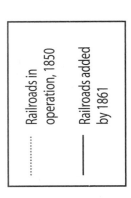

Map #: 085

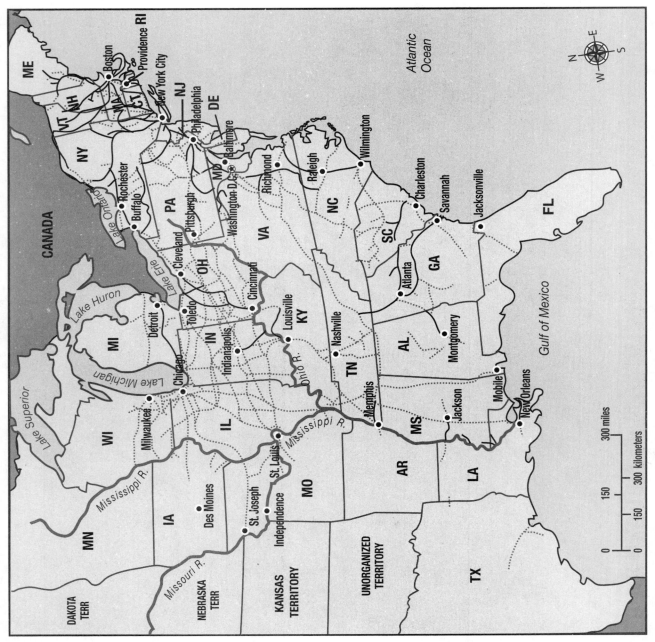

Railroads in operation, 1850

Railroads added by 1861

Name: _____

Date: _____

States Secede From the Union

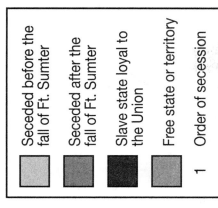

Map #: 086

☐	Seceded before the fall of Ft. Sumter
☐	Seceded after the fall of Ft. Sumter
■	Slave state loyal to the Union
☐	Free state or territory
1	Order of secession

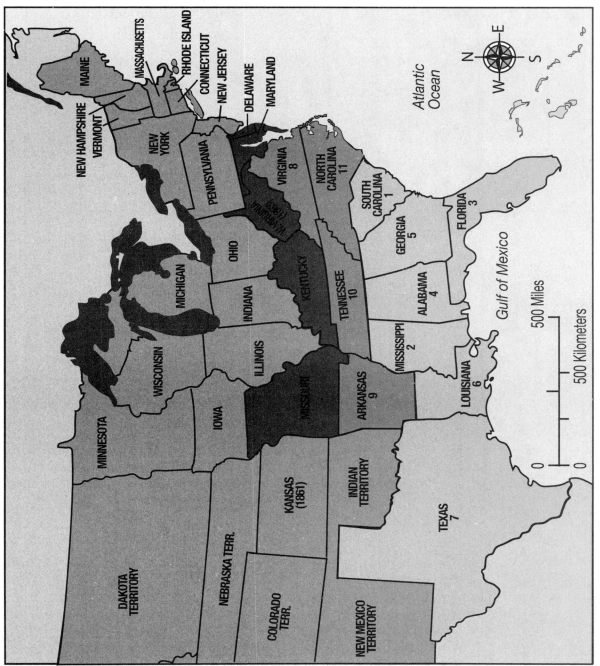

Name: _____

Date: _____

Union and Confederate States

Union states
Confederate states
Union territories
Border states

ME.

N.H.

VT.

MASS.

R.I.

CONN.

N.Y.

N.J.

PA.

DEL.

MD.

W.VA. (1863)

VA.

N.C.

S.C.

FLA.

OHIO

IND.

KY.

TENN.

GA.

ALA.

MICH.

ILL.

MISS.

WIS.

MO.

ARK.

LA.

IOWA

MINN.

KANSAS (1861)

INDIAN TERRITORY

TEXAS

DAKOTA TERRITORY

NEBRASKA TERR.

COLORADO TERR.

NEW MEXICO TERRITORY

WASHINGTON TERRITORY

UTAH TERR.

OREGON

NEV. TERR.

CALIFORNIA

500 Miles

500 Kilometers

0

Name: _____

Date: _____

Civil War Strategy

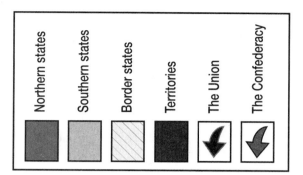

Northern states

Southern states

Border states

Territories

The Union

The Confederacy

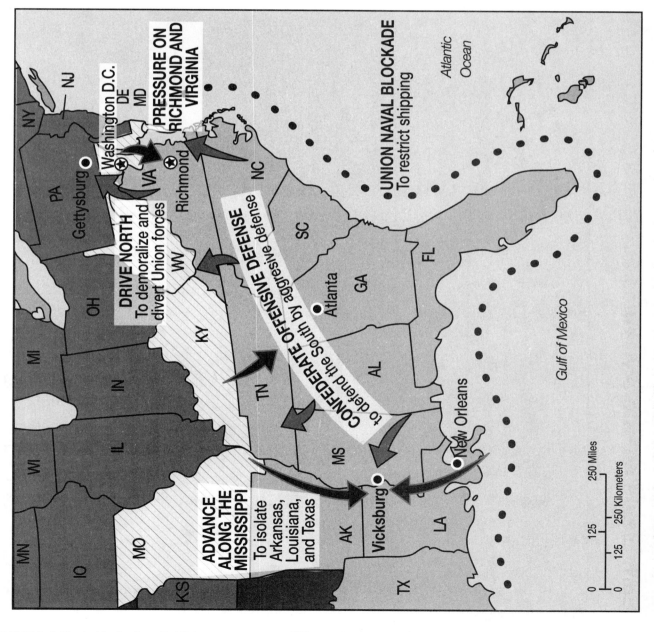

PRESSURE ON RICHMOND AND VIRGINIA

Washington D.C.
DE
MD

NJ

NY

PA

Gettysburg

VA

Richmond

WV

NC

DRIVE NORTH
To demoralize and divert Union forces

OH

KY

SC

UNION NAVAL BLOCKADE
To restrict shipping

Atlantic Ocean

CONFEDERATE OFFENSIVE DEFENSE
to defend the South by aggresive defense

MI

IN

TN

Atlanta

GA

AL

FL

WI

IL

MS

New Orleans

Gulf of Mexico

MN

IO

MO

ADVANCE ALONG THE MISSISSIPPI
To isolate Arkansas, Louisiana, and Texas

KS

AK

Vicksburg

LA

TX

250 Miles

250 Kilometers

125

125

0

0

Map #: 089

Name: _____

Date: _____

Early Battles of the Civil War, 1861–1862

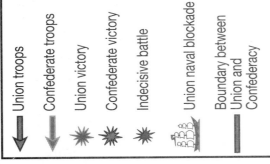

- Union troops
- Confederate troops
- Union victory
- Confederate victory
- Indecisive battle
- Union naval blockade
- Boundary between Union and Confederacy

1. Ft. Sumter falls to Confederate troops.
2. Union blockade cuts Confederate flow of trade and supplies.
3. With about 23,000 casualties, Shiloh is the bloodiest battle fought thus far.
4. Antietam costs more casualties than any other single day of the war—over 23,000 killed or wounded.

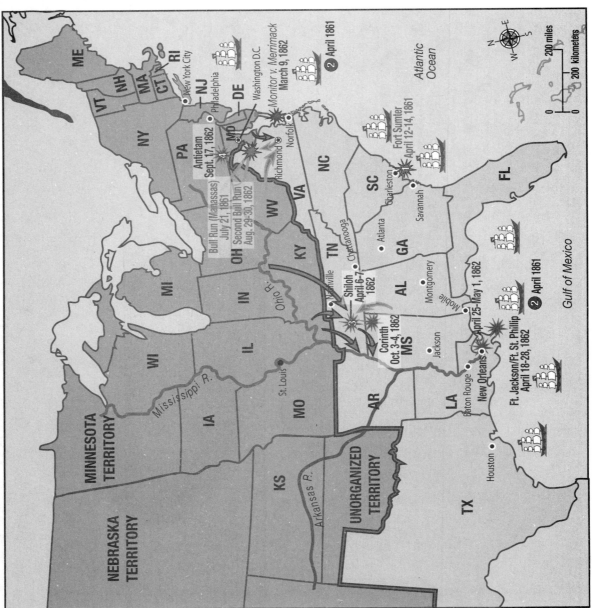

ME
NH
VT
MA
CT
RI
NY
NJ
PA
DE
MD
Washington D.C.
New York City
Philadelphia

Antietam
Sept. 17, 1862

Bull Run (Manassas)
July 21, 1861
Second Bull Run
Aug. 29–30, 1862

Monitor v. Merrimack
March 9, 1862

2 April 1861

Norfolk
Richmond
WV
VA
NC
SC
Charleston
Savannah

Fort Sumter
April 12–14, 1861

Atlantic Ocean

OH
IN
IL
MI
WI
IA

KY
TN
Nashville
Chattanooga
Atlanta
GA
AL
Montgomery
Mobile
Shiloh
April 6–7, 1862
Corinth
Oct. 3–4, 1862
MS
Jackson

FL

Gulf of Mexico

2 April 1861

Ohio R.
Mississippi R.
St. Louis
MO
AR
Arkansas R.

LA
Baton Rouge
New Orleans
April 25–May 1, 1862
Ft. Jackson/Ft. St. Phillip
April 18–28, 1862

KS
UNORGANIZED TERRITORY
TX
Houston

MINNESOTA TERRITORY
NEBRASKA TERRITORY

N E S W

0   200 miles
0   200 kilometers

Name: _____

Date: _____

Civil War Battles, 1862–1863

Union troops

Confederate troops

Union victory

Confederate victory

Indecisive battle

Union naval blockade

Boundary between Union and Confederacy

Union victories at Vicksburg & Gettysburg marked the turning point of the Civil War.

Siege of Vicksburg ends with a Confederate surrender; Union isolates western Confederacy.

After Gettysburg, southern troops never again penetrate so deeply into Union territory.

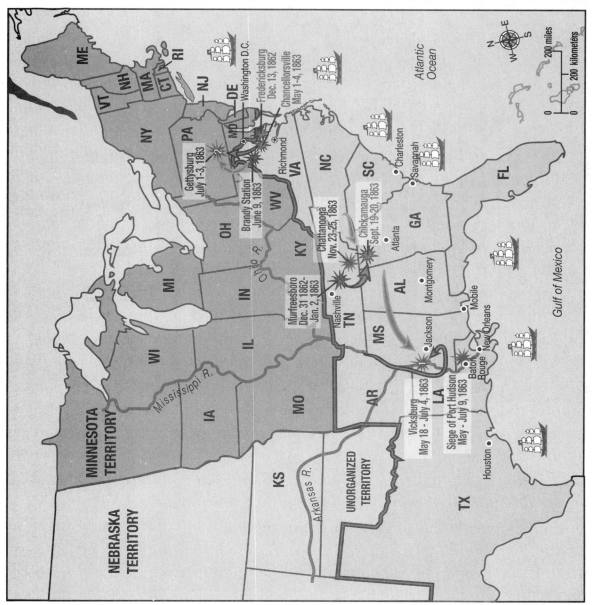

Name: _____ Date: _____

Battle of Gettysburg

Map #: 091

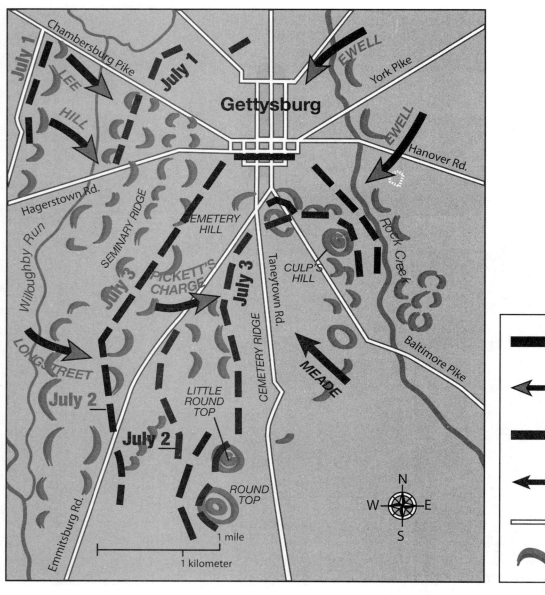

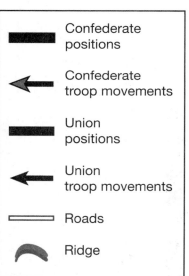

Name: _____

Date: _____

Final Civil War Battles, 1864–1865

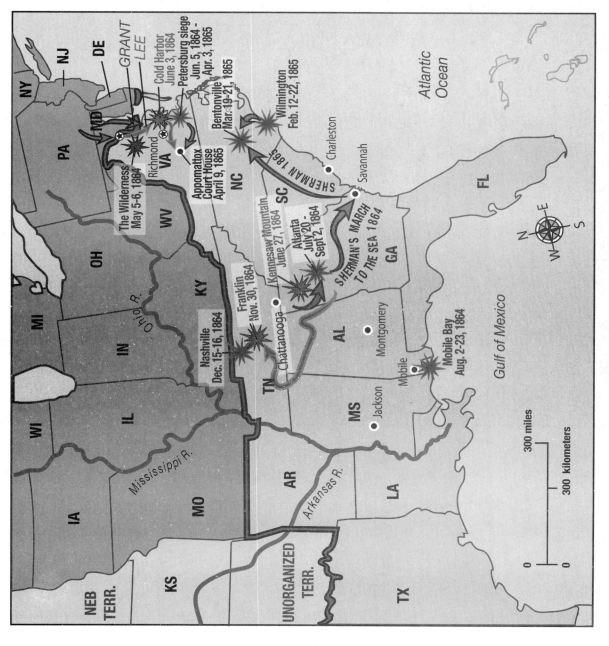

Legend:
- Union troops
- Confederate troops
- Union victory
- Confederate victory
- Indecisive battle
- Boundary between Union and Confederacy

The Wilderness May 5-6, 1864
Richmond
GRANT
LEE
Cold Harbor June 3, 1864
Petersburg siege Jun. 5, 1864 – Apr. 3, 1865
Appomattox Court House April 9, 1865
Bentonville Mar. 19-21, 1865
Wilmington Feb. 12-22, 1865
Charleston
Savannah
SHERMAN 1865
SHERMAN'S MARCH TO THE SEA 1864
Kennesaw Mountain June 27, 1864
Atlanta July 20 – Sept 2, 1864
Franklin Nov. 30, 1864
Nashville Dec. 15-16, 1864
Chattanooga
Montgomery
Mobile
Mobile Bay Aug. 2-23, 1864
Jackson

NEB. TERR.
KS
IA
MO
WI
IL
IN
MI
OH
KY
TN
AR
MS
AL
GA
FL
LA
TX
UNORGANIZED TERR.
NY
PA
NJ
DE
MD
WV
VA
NC
SC

Mississippi R.
Ohio R.
Arkansas R.
Gulf of Mexico
Atlantic Ocean

N E W S

300 miles
300 kilometers

Name: _____

Date: _____

Reconstruction: Dates of Readmission to the Union and Reestablished Conservative Governments

Map #: 093

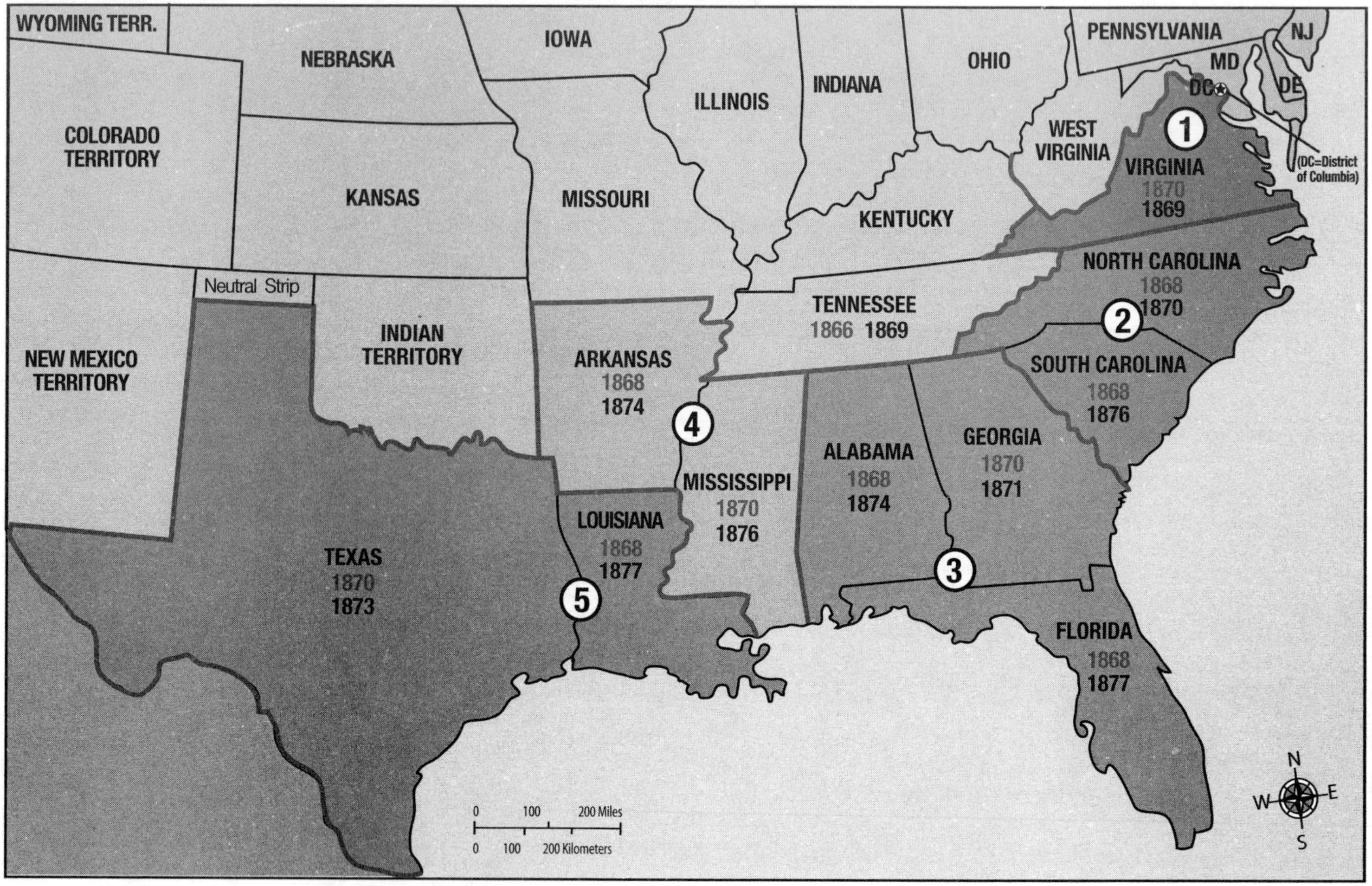

Legend:

- Military districts established March, 1867
- 1868 Dates indicate readmission to the Union
- 1874 Dates indicate reestablishment of conservative government

WYOMING TERR.

NEBRASKA

IOWA

COLORADO TERRITORY

KANSAS

MISSOURI

ILLINOIS

INDIANA

OHIO

PENNSYLVANIA

NJ

DE

MD

DC—District of Columbia

NEW MEXICO TERRITORY

INDIAN TERRITORY

Neutral Strip

ARKANSAS 1868 1874

TENNESSEE 1866 1869

KENTUCKY

WEST VIRGINIA

VIRGINIA 1870 1869

NORTH CAROLINA 1868 1870

SOUTH CAROLINA 1868 1876

GEORGIA 1870 1871

ALABAMA 1868 1874

MISSISSIPPI 1870 1876

LOUISIANA 1868 1877

TEXAS 1870 1873

FLORIDA 1868 1877

1 2 3 4 5

N E S W

0 100 200 Miles
0 100 200 Kilometers

Major Indian War Battles, 1860–1890

Map #: 094

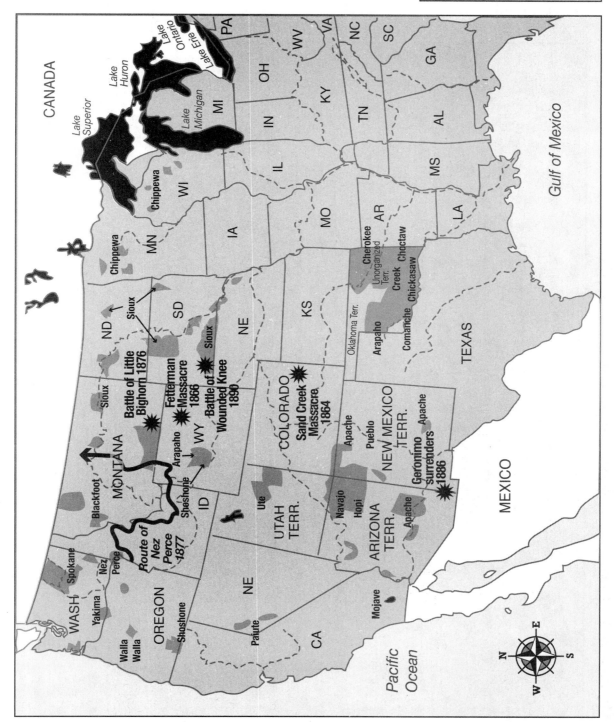

Name: _____

Date: _____

The Chisholm and Other Cattle Trails of the Western United States

Map #: 095

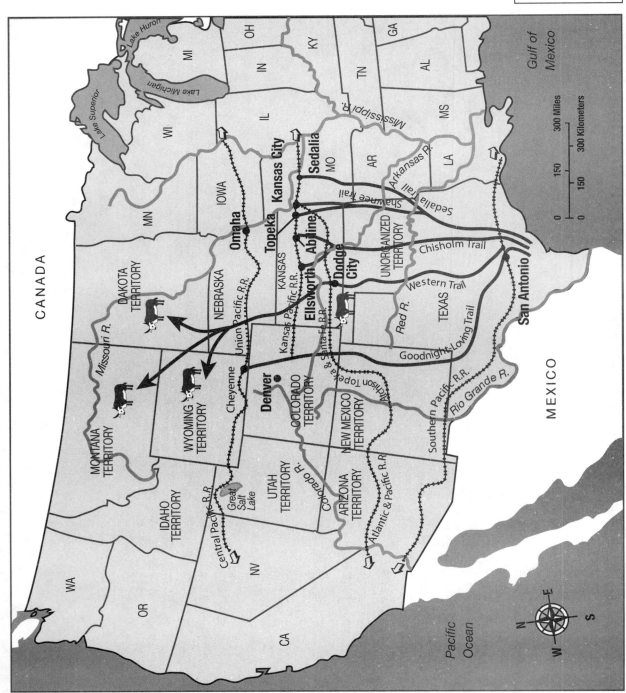

Name: _____

Date: _____

States and Territories of the United States, 1868–1876

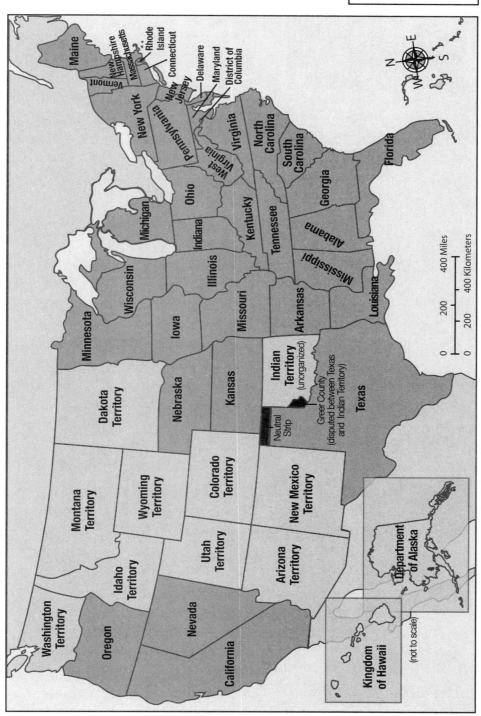

Legend:
- States
- Territories
- Other countries
- Disputed areas

400 Miles

400 Kilometers

Name: _____

Date: _____

Transcontinental Railroad

Omaha

Mississippi R.

Platte R.

Cheyenne

UNION PACIFIC

Promontory

Ogden

CENTRAL PACIFIC

Great Salt Lake

Salt Lake City

Colorado R.

Humboldt R.

Reno

Sacramento

San Francisco

0   150   300 Miles

0   150   300 Kilometers

Name: _____

Date: _____

Railroad Growth, 1870–1890

Railroad Growth
Between 1870–1890

—— Major rail lines
in 1870

—— Major rail lines
added 1870–1890

PACIFIC
TIME ZONE

MOUNTAIN
TIME ZONE

CENTRAL
TIME ZONE

EASTERN
TIME ZONE

Seattle

Portland

San Francisco

Los Angeles

Salt Lake City

Denver

El Paso

Dallas

Omaha

Kansas City

Minneapolis-
St. Paul

St. Louis

Chicago

Memphis

New Orleans

Detroit

Cleveland

Cincinnati

Atlanta

Charleston

Buffalo

Pittsburgh

Washington, D.C.

New York

Boston

Pacific
Ocean

Atlantic
Ocean

Gulf of Mexico

N
W E
S

0   200   400 Miles

0   200   400 Kilometers

Name: _____

Date: _____

Railroads and Growth in the West, 1890

Map #: 099

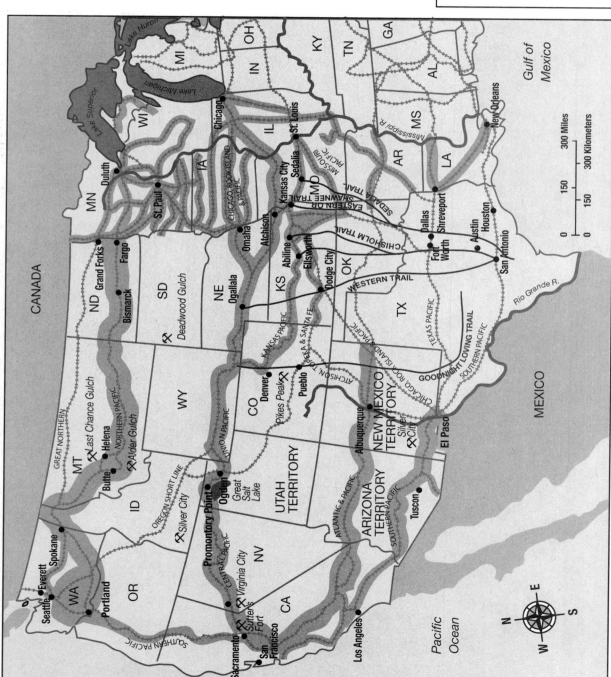

Legend:
- Railroads in 1890
- Cattle trails
- Railroad land grants
- Mining centers

Map #: 100

Name: _____

Date: _____

Western Land Use, 1890

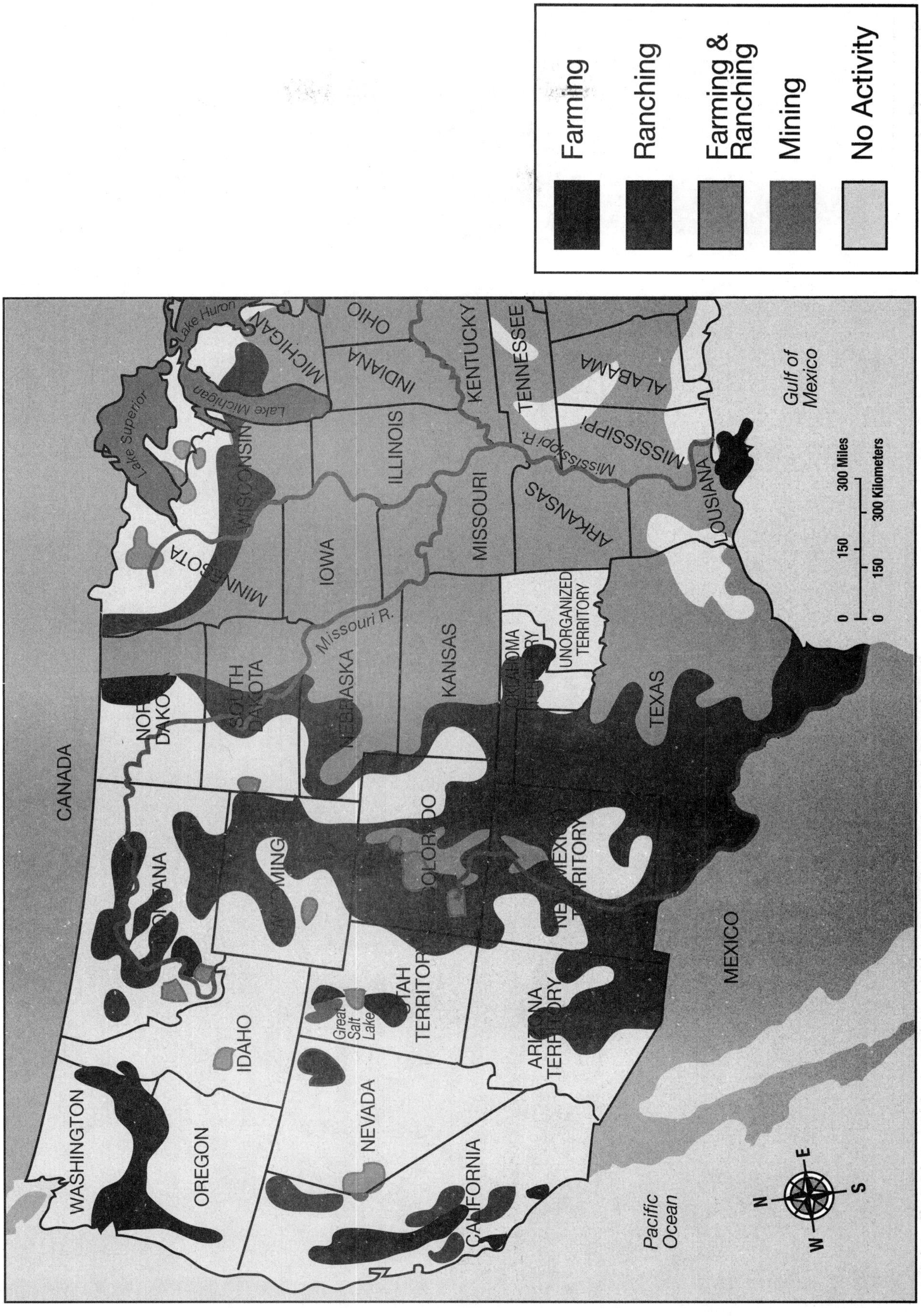

Farming

Ranching

Farming & Ranching

Mining

No Activity

Name: _____

Date: _____

Immigration, 1870–1900

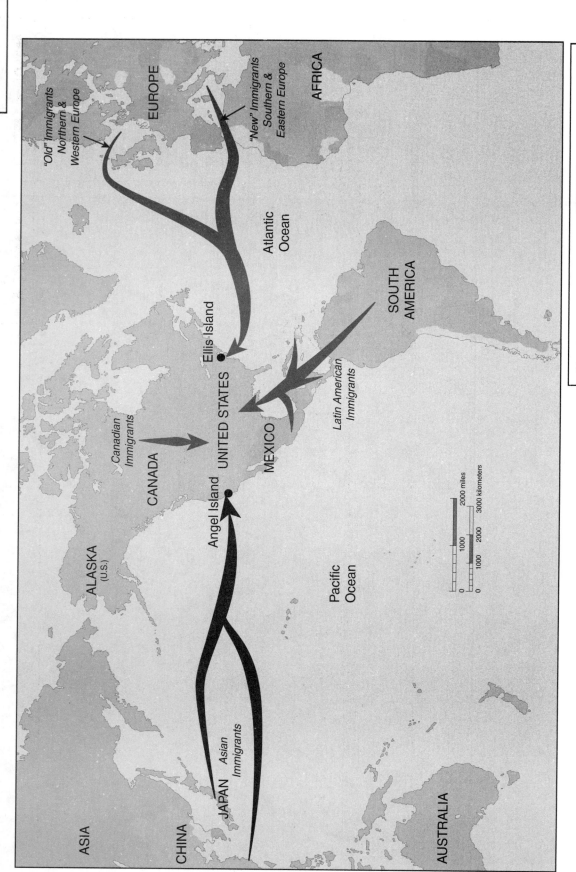

EUROPE

"Old" Immigrants
Northern &
Western Europe

"New" Immigrants
Southern &
Eastern Europe

AFRICA

Atlantic
Ocean

SOUTH
AMERICA

Latin American
Immigrants

Ellis Island

UNITED STATES

MEXICO

Canadian
Immigrants

CANADA

ALASKA
(U.S.)

Angel Island

Pacific
Ocean

ASIA

CHINA

JAPAN

Asian
Immigrants

AUSTRALIA

0   1000   2000 miles

0   1000   2000   3000 kilometers

Number of Immigrants,
Highest to Lowest

Europe

Canada

Asia

Latin America

Name: ______________________ Date: ______________________

Labor Strikes, 1870–1900

Map #: 102

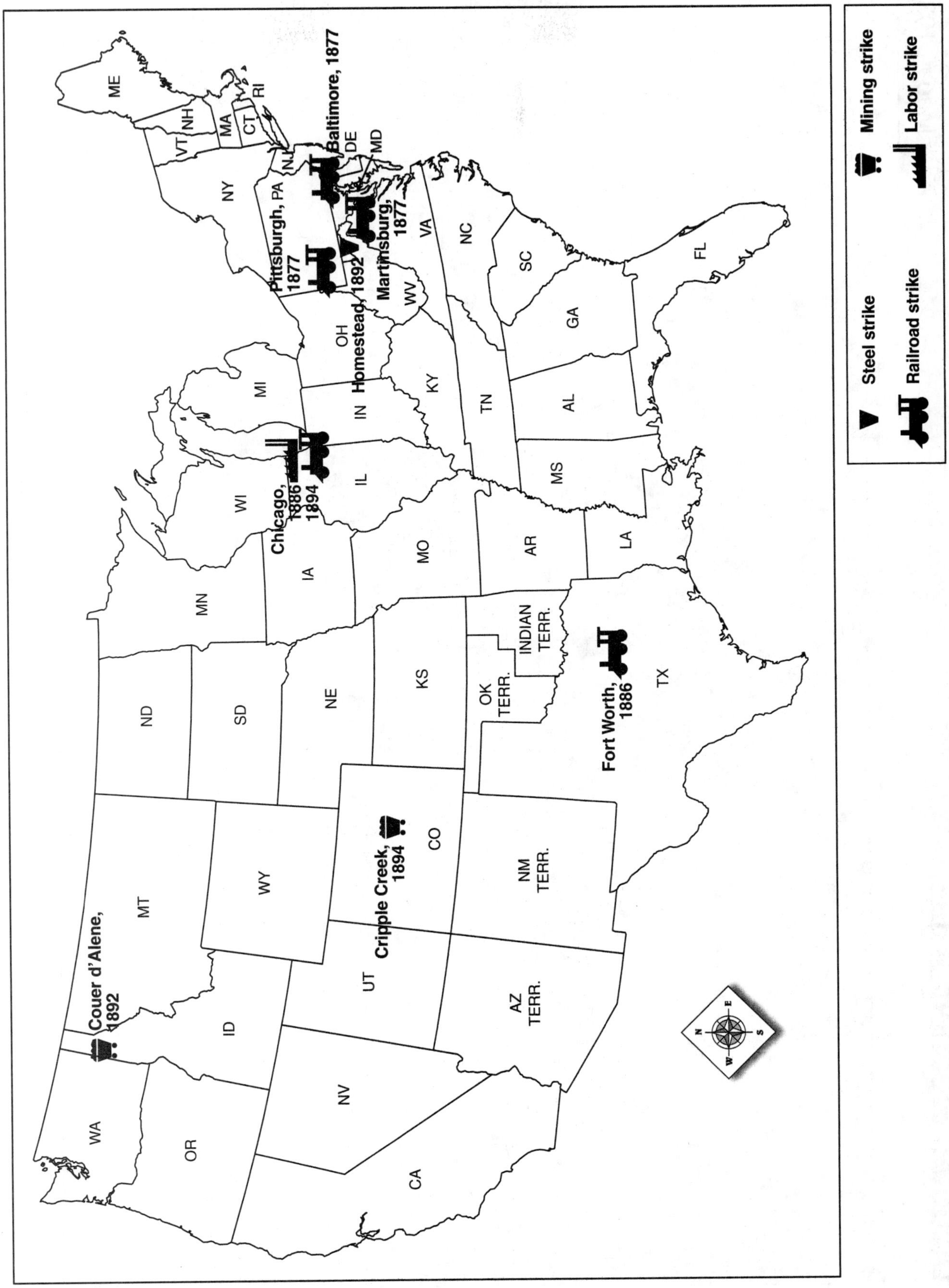
Couer d'Alene, 1892
Cripple Creek, 1894
Fort Worth, 1886
Chicago, 1886 1894
Homestead, 1892
Pittsburgh, PA 1877
Martinsburg, 1877
Baltimore, 1877
ME
NH
VT
MA
CT
RI
NY
NJ
PA
DE
MD
VA
WV
NC
SC
GA
FL
OH
MI
IN
KY
TN
AL
MS
IL
WI
IA
MO
AR
LA
MN
ND
SD
NE
KS
INDIAN TERR.
OK TERR.
TX
MT
WY
CO
NM TERR.
ID
UT
AZ TERR.
WA
OR
NV
CA
N
E
S
W
Mining strike
Labor strike
Steel strike
Railroad strike

Name: _____

Date: _____

Disputed Election of 1876

Map #: 103

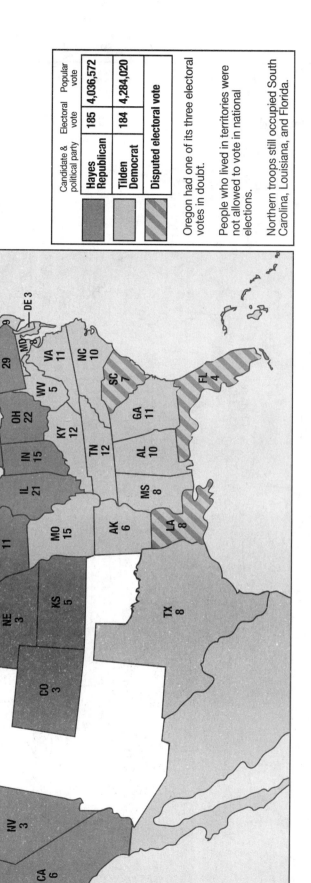

Candidate & political party	Electoral vote	Popular vote
Hayes Republican	185	4,036,572
Tilden Democrat	184	4,284,020
Disputed electoral vote		

Oregon had one of its three electoral votes in doubt.

People who lived in territories were not allowed to vote in national elections.

Northern troops still occupied South Carolina, Louisiana, and Florida.

ME 7

VT 5

NH 5

MA 13

CT 6

RI 4

NY 35

NJ 9

DE 3

PA 29

MD 8

VA 11

NC 10

WV 5

SC 7

FL 4

OH 22

KY 12

GA 11

MI 11

IN 15

TN 12

AL 10

IL 21

MS 8

WI 10

AK 6

LA 8

IA 11

MO 15

MN 5

KS 5

TX 8

NE 3

CO 3

TERRITORIES

NV 3

OR 2

CA 6

Map #: 104

Name: _____

Date: _____

Major Industrial Areas, 1890

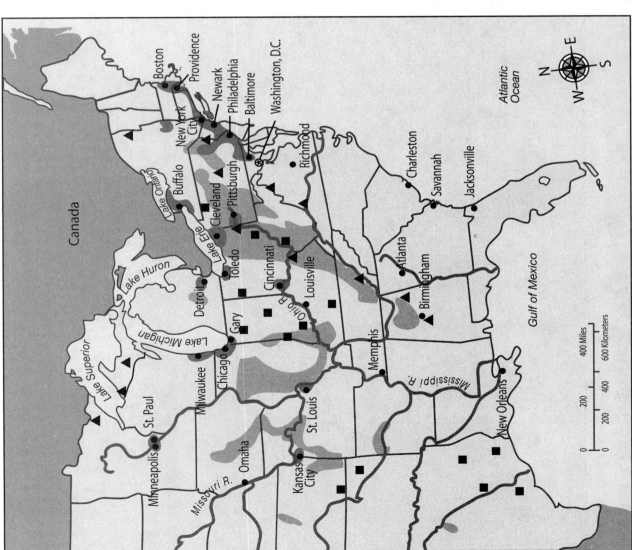

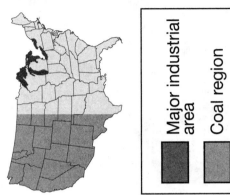

Legend:
- Major industrial area
- Coal region
- Iron region ▲
- Oil region ■

Name: _____   Date: _____

Routes of the Klondike Gold Rush

Map #: 105

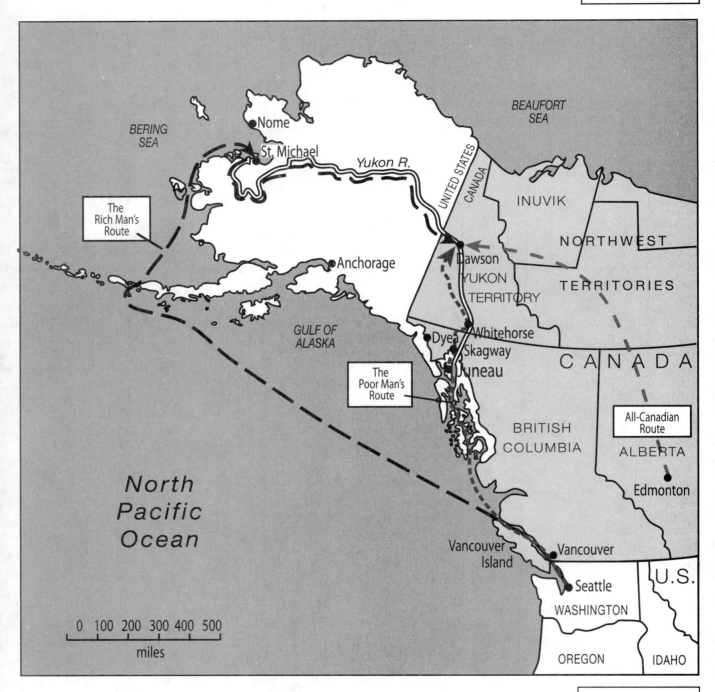

The Rich Man's Route

The Poor Man's Route

All-Canadian Route

BERING SEA

BEAUFORT SEA

Nome

St. Michael

Yukon R.

UNITED STATES

CANADA

INUVIK

NORTHWEST

TERRITORIES

Anchorage

Dawson

YUKON TERRITORY

GULF OF ALASKA

Dyea

Whitehorse

Skagway

Juneau

CANADA

BRITISH COLUMBIA

ALBERTA

Edmonton

North Pacific Ocean

Vancouver Island

Vancouver

Seattle

U.S.

WASHINGTON

OREGON

IDAHO

0 100 200 300 400 500
miles

The Rich Man's Route
(All Water Route)

The Poor Man's Route

The All-Canadian Route

Name: _____

Date: _____

Spanish-American War

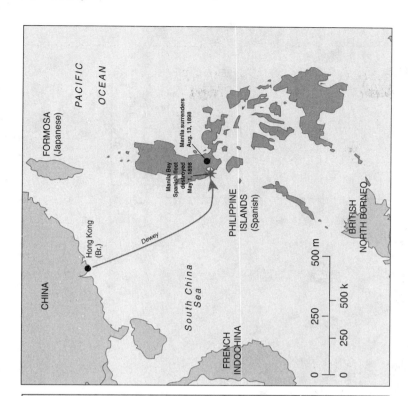

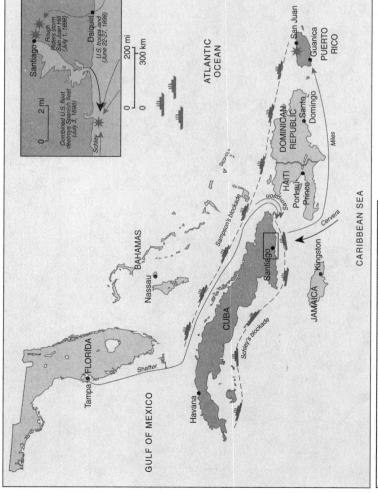

PACIFIC OCEAN

FORMOSA (Japanese)

CHINA

Hong Kong (Br.)

Dewey

South China Sea

FRENCH INDOCHINA

PHILIPPINE ISLANDS (Spanish)

Manila Bay Spanish fleet destroyed May 1, 1898

Manila surrenders Aug. 13, 1898

BRITISH NORTH BORNEO

500 m

500 k

250

250

0

0

GULF OF MEXICO

Tampa FLORIDA

Shafter

Havana

CUBA

Schley's blockade

BAHAMAS

Nassau

Sampson's blockade

ATLANTIC OCEAN

HAITI

Port-au-Prince

Santo Domingo

DOMINICAN REPUBLIC

Miles

San Juan

Guanica

PUERTO RICO

Cervera

JAMAICA

Kingston

CARIBBEAN SEA

Santiago

Santiago

Rough Riders storm San Juan Hill (July 1, 1898)

Daiquiri

U.S. troops land (June 22-27, 1898)

Combined U.S. fleet destroys Spanish fleet (July 3, 1898)

Schley

2 mi

0

200 mi

300 km

0

Spanish territory

Other areas

U.S. forces

U.S. victories

Spanish forces

U.S. naval blockade

Name: _____

Date: _____

Voting Rights for Women, 1919

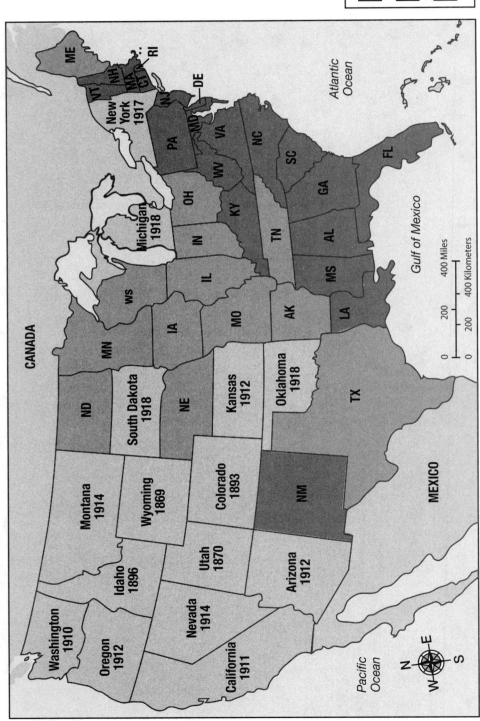

Equal suffrage, date effective

Partial suffrage

No statewide suffrage

CANADA

Washington 1910
Oregon 1912
California 1911
Nevada 1914
Idaho 1896
Montana 1914
Wyoming 1869
Utah 1870
Arizona 1912
Colorado 1893
NM
ND
South Dakota 1918
NE
Kansas 1912
Oklahoma 1918
TX
MEXICO

MN
WS
IA
MO
AK
LA
MS
AL
GA
FL

IL
IN
OH
KY
TN

Michigan 1918

New York 1917
VT
NH
MA
CT
RI
ME
NJ
PA
MD
DE
WV
VA
NC
SC

Atlantic Ocean

Gulf of Mexico

Pacific Ocean

N E S W

0 200 400 Miles
0 200 400 Kilometers

Name: _____

Date: _____

Percentage of Persons Receiving Unemployment Relief by State, 1934

Map #: 108

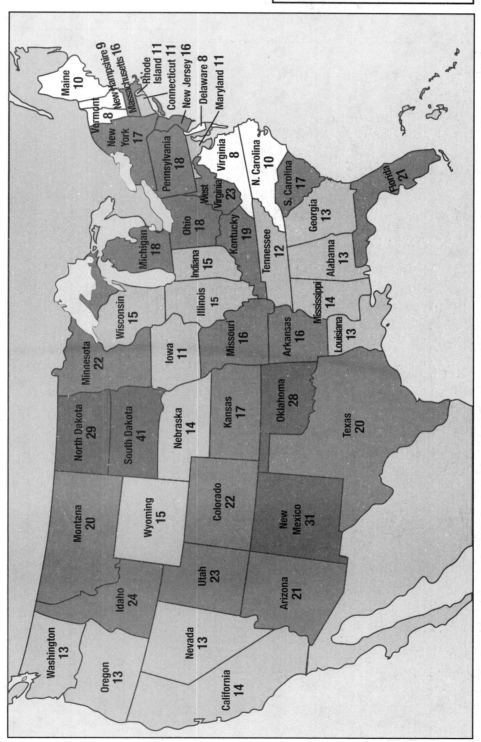

Persons receiving unemployment relief in 1934 as % of state population

- 26 - above
- 16 - 25
- 11 - 15
- 0 - 10

Maine 10
New Hampshire 9
Vermont 8
Massachusetts 16
Rhode Island 11
Connecticut 11
New Jersey 16
Delaware 8
Maryland 11
New York 17
Pennsylvania 18
Virginia 8
West Virginia 23
N. Carolina 10
Ohio 18
Kentucky 19
Tennessee 12
S. Carolina 17
Georgia 13
Florida 21
Michigan 18
Indiana 15
Illinois 15
Missouri 16
Arkansas 16
Alabama 13
Mississippi 14
Louisiana 13
Wisconsin 15
Iowa 11
Minnesota 22
North Dakota 29
South Dakota 41
Nebraska 14
Kansas 17
Oklahoma 28
Texas 20
Montana 20
Wyoming 15
Colorado 22
New Mexico 31
Idaho 24
Utah 23
Arizona 21
Washington 13
Oregon 13
Nevada 13
California 14

Name: _____

Date: _____

Dust Bowl, 1930s

Map #: 109

Area most affected by Dust Bowl conditions

ME

VT

NH

MA

CT

RI

NY

NJ

DE

MD

PA

WV

VA

NC

SC

FL

OH

KY

TN

GA

AL

MI

IN

MS

IL

WI

MO

AR

LA

IA

Oklahoma City

OK

MN

Topeka

KS

TX

Austin

ND

SD

NE

Denver

CO

Santa Fe

NM

MT

WY

UT

AZ

ID

NV

WA

OR

CA

N E
W S

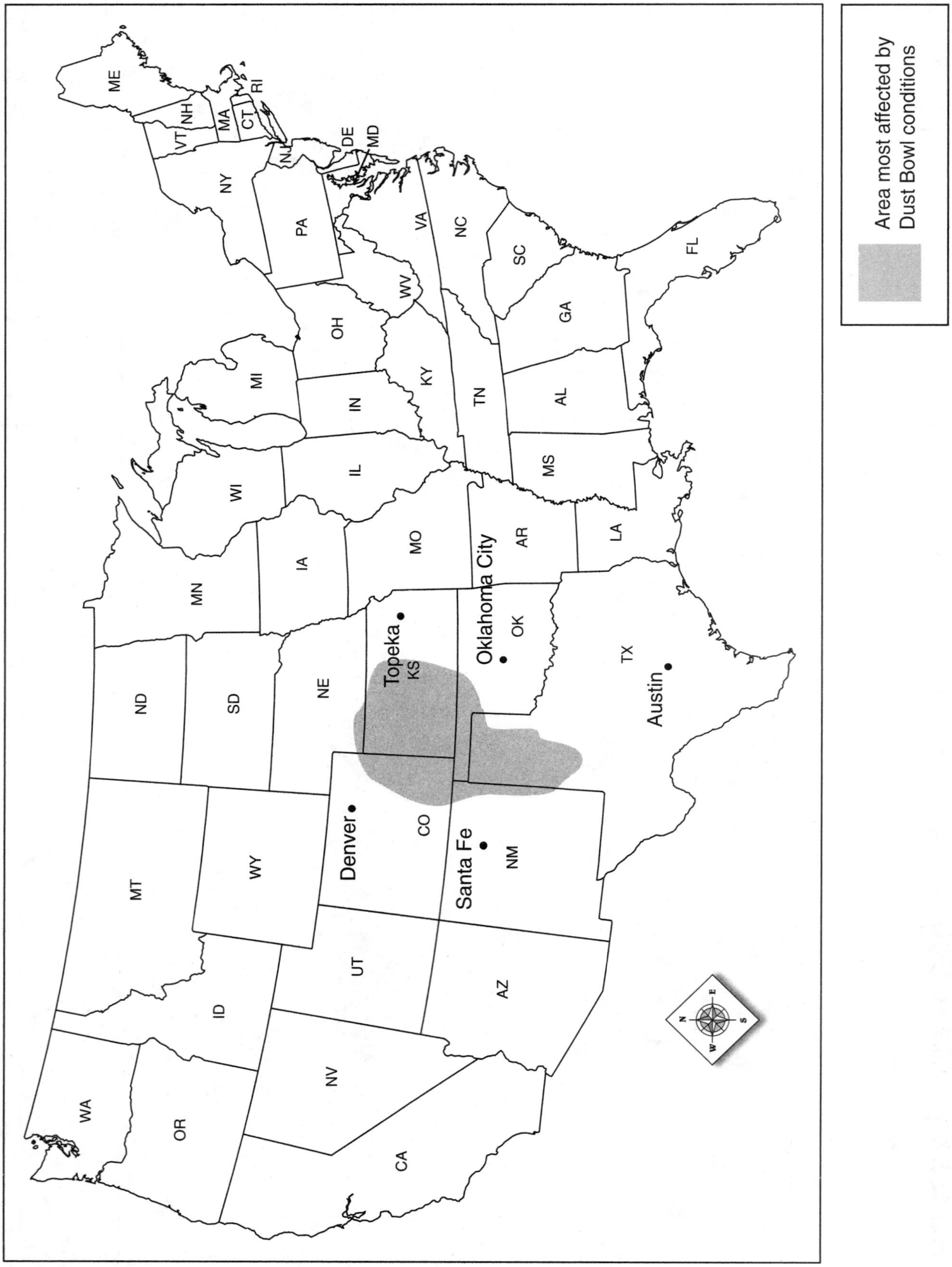

Name: _____

Date: _____

Route 66, 1926–1985

Map #: 110

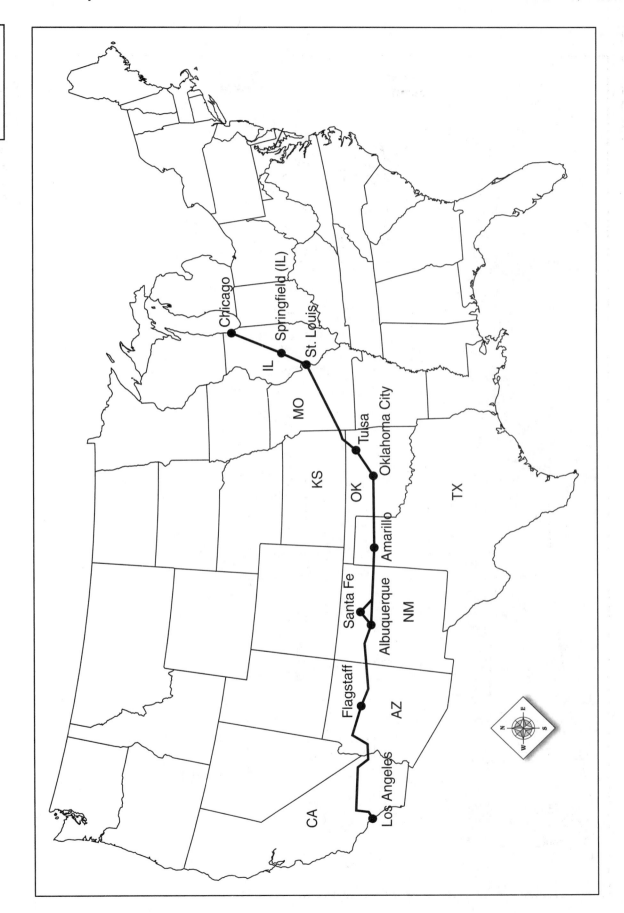

Name: _____

Date: _____

Electoral College Map

Map #: 111

Winner takes all electors

Elector count may be split

Total electoral votes: 538

Majority needed to win: 270

Name: _____

Date: _____

Location of the United States Mints

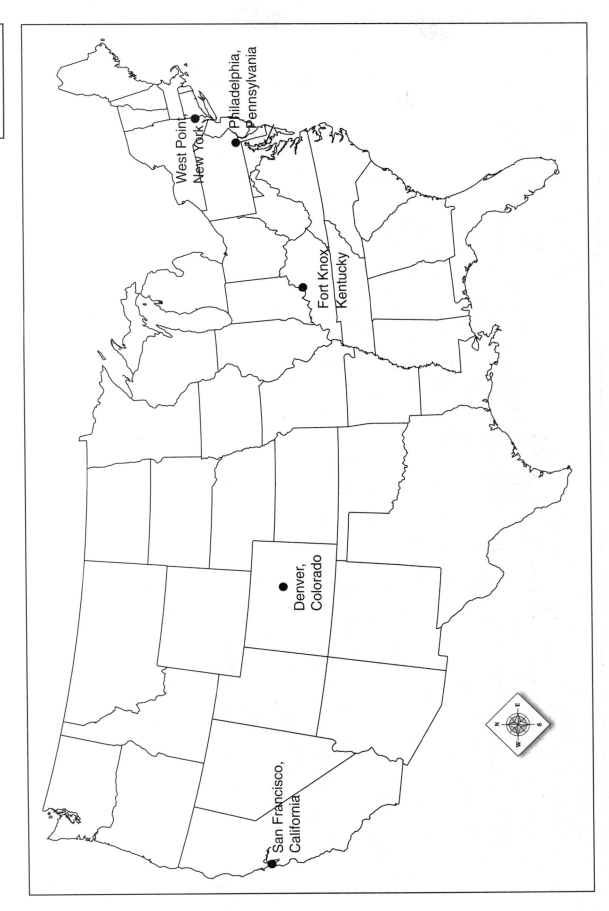

West Point,
New York

Philadelphia,
Pennsylvania

Fort Knox,
Kentucky

Denver,
Colorado

San Francisco,
California

Name: ______________________ Date: ______________________

Climate Regions of the United States

Map #: 113

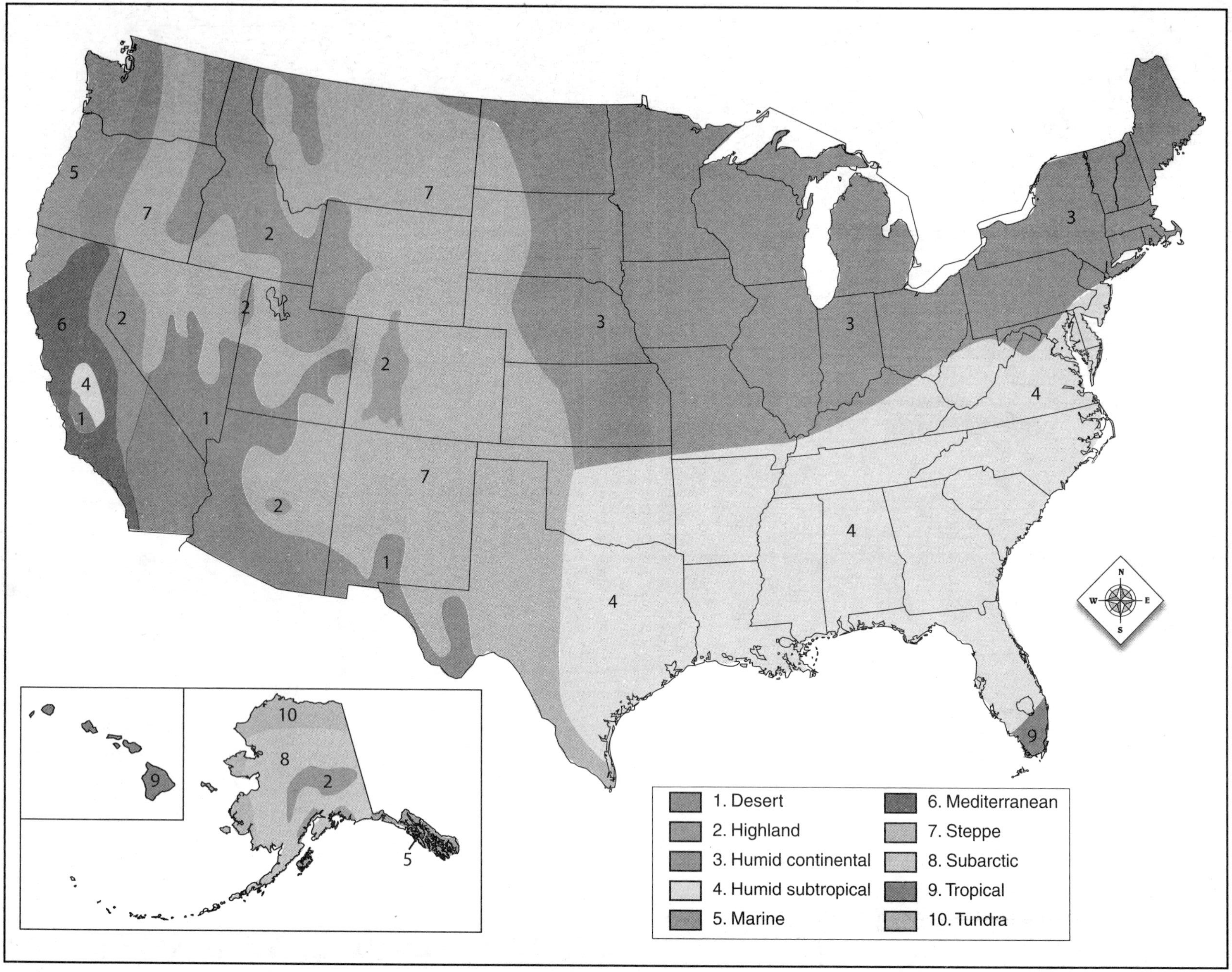
5
7
7
2
6
2
2
4
1
1
2
3
3
3
2
7
1
4
4
4
9
10
8
2
9
5
N
W
E
S
1. Desert
2. Highland
3. Humid continental
4. Humid subtropical
5. Marine
6. Mediterranean
7. Steppe
8. Subarctic
9. Tropical
10. Tundra